Faeries

of the

Wild, Wild
Moon

Faeries
of the
Wild, Wild
Moon

Vivienne Manouge

WELLMAN BOOKS

Wellman Books
PO Box 466
Chester, Nova Scotia
Canada
B0J 1J0
www.wellmanbooks.com

First Edition

Canadian Cataloguing in Publication Data

Manouge, Vivienne, 1951-
Faeries of the wild, wild moon
ISBN 0-9681940-3-6
1. Fairies. I. Title
BF1552.M35 2001   133.1'4   C2001-901875-4

Acknowledgements

Grateful thanks to Helen Sutanovic who read and then re-read every word, and to my mother, whose quiet love sustained me through it all. My thanks and admiration go to publisher Matthew Scott, who wrestled it into shape with great strength and vision, and not less to Susanne Marshall for her sensitive and creative editing. To Philip Carr-Gomm, for his thoughtful introduction, my gratitude. My grateful thanks and love go also to the many faerie spirits and other extradimensional beings who helped to bring this book into the world. Last but not least, thanks and blessings to you the reader, whose perennial love for the faerie folk is the real reason this book was written.

For Wendy - who helped.

Foreword

Here is a deceptively brief book—an autobiography—an account of a spiritual odyssey—that has an enticing directness. It deals with one of the most romantic areas of life here on earth, an area that lures many of us, that tantalises children, that inspires artists and poets. And yet despite the romance of its theme, the existence of faeries, this book shows the author determined to be straight with us, determined to recount what has happened to her without distortion. I believe her life depends on this, her honesty, because to deceive herself or us would plunge her into a world of insanity she has so very nearly entered in the extraordinary adventure she has undertaken.

This adventure has been nothing less than exploring the nature and identity of faeries. As a child Vivienne asked herself the question perhaps every sensitive child asks: "Who and what are 'faeries' exactly?" But whereas most of us give up asking this question, she didn't - or the faeries didn't let her. And as you shall discover as you turn the pages of this book, the consequences of her holding this question in her heart for so long has cost Vivienne her health, and I sense has nearly cost her her life and her sanity.

She was able to preserve her sanity and her life in the end by applying her own advice: "People who are seeing them (fairies) must give as honest and complete an account of what they see as they can, to anyone who seems likely to give it intelligent and open minded attention. Not only does this pave the way for a further thinning of the veil, but it will also turn some people's attention to their own psychic perceptions, and help them to focus on the faeries in their own lives so that they may improve their rapport until the communion becomes conscious for them, too." By recounting what she saw and felt and was told, she has been able to give to others the gifts of faery-knowledge she obtained at such cost over so many years. The answers she found to the questions she asked are not perhaps the ones you might expect. She found herself conversing with a very specific kind of Being, and learned how they come into existence, where they come from and what their function is. Years ago I might have doubted the possibility of such beings existing, were it not for an experience I had in Ireland, which I will never forget.

Olivia Durdin-Robertson, who founded the Fellowship of Isis with her brother Lawrence, had developed a method of exploring the Otherworld, which she called by the unassuming term 'guided meditation'. I have since discovered that two researchers, one in Australia, and another in America, had been simultaneously developing a similar method. Steven Glaskin in Australia called it the 'Christos' technique, and wrote about it in a number of books, including 'Windows of the Mind'. Olivia's method involved an 'operator' and a 'percipient'. The operator performed a simple ceremony at the beginning and end of the experience, applied spiritual healing, and acted as a guide to the percipient, who was sent on a voyage into the Otherworld, into other states of Being.

I was lucky enough to spend six months or more at Olivia's home, Huntington Castle, and during this time she sent me on many voyages into the Otherworld, and taught me how to send others on such voyages too. Helped by an initial session of spiritual healing and an opening ceremony that created a strong feeling of blessing and protection, I would lie for hours at a time, several evenings a week, on a couch in the old library of the castle. Olivia would then guide me on a meditation, leading me on a journey which would begin in the realm of the imagination, or creative visualisation, but which would change, at a certain moment, to become a journey through an entirely different realm: an Otherworldly land peopled by other intelligencies. Sometimes we seemed to travel into the past to converse with beings from other times or to enter past lives. Other times we seemed to travel into the future, and to other levels of Reality hard to describe in words. And at one time I was taken to meet a Being who was a fire elemental, deva or salamander: he rose out of an ancient temple-tomb and was vast, maybe a hundred feet high. He was made of shining gold and red fire-light, which shimmered and radiated. We communicated, but not with words, and I can understand fully why it has taken Vivienne so long to write about her communications with beings who, like this nature-spirit, have such a different consciousness to humans. It would make it even harder to believe in faeries, if we had to accept that they had somehow learned human languages.

This experience convinced me that there are indeed beings that we call by such names as elementals, elves, and fairies. And it showed me that we can communicate with them, as long as we let go of our need to use external conversation as our medium. For years afterwards, though, I was entranced by the thought that such beings existed, and it took a while to come to the realisation expressed so clearly by Vivienne, when she says: "We humans tend to think of ourselves as great lumps of materiality, slow-witted, dull-sensed, unmagical, and powerless, at least compared with faeries and elementals and their ilk. In fact, we are every bit as magical as they are, if only we could wake up to it."

In some exciting, and hardly comprehensible way, it seems that we as humans are destined to work together

x

with such beings, and the first stage in this process requires us to recognise that they actually exist, and that we can communicate with them.

To do this, we must use the web of life itself. We must learn to trust the fact that in some amazing, and as yet inexplicable way the natural world of trees, plants, flowers and crystals are able to transmit messages, signals, and even, as Vivienne describes, the faeries themselves: "Eventually she could reach any individual flower in the biome reasonably rapidly from any other flower anywhere on Earth, scrolling through till she found the location you wanted. Since distance is no object, what about other planets? Theoretically, she could locate, scroll her way through to, and emerge from, any flower on any plant anywhere in the universe as easily as you can now make a phone call, except it's not just your voice you would transmit, it's yourself."

Any doubt of mine that such a web existed was removed for me one day in Holland. I was leading a workshop on the tree-lore of the Druids, and we were about to enter a forest to commune with the trees, when a woman collapsed in tears. She explained that it was her granddaughter's birthday, but that she had become estranged from her daughter, who would not let her communicate with her grandchild. This caused her immense pain, and it had suddenly overwhelmed her. I talked to her about the idea of the web of life, and about the way Druids and indigenous peoples believe that we can use trees as telephones to talk to each other at great distances. "It seems crazy," I told her, "but try it! See if you can send a message to your granddaughter through a tree."

We then fanned out into the forest, each of us picking a tree which seemed right for us, to perform our meditative exercise. An hour later we gathered together to compare notes. The grandmother began crying again. But this time she was crying for joy. She explained that she hadn't been able to find a tree that really felt right, so picked instead a strong, handsome looking tree to lean against. As she began the exercise she seemed to feel the tree saying "It's not me you need" and then she started to sense a nearby tree communicating with her, saying: "Come here. Sit by me. I can help you." Her rational mind thought this absurd, and the tree itself was unattractive to her - small and scrawny. But in the end the call was so insistent, she moved, and began the exercise again with this new tree. She entered into a feeling of deep communion with the tree; somehow she knew she was meant to be with it. She then sent a message to her granddaughter: "Happy Birthday! I love you!"

In a while, she sensed the tree telling her that it had a gift for her: "Open your eyes and look down" it said. She did so, and found herself looking at what she thought was a bright red autumn leaf. She stretched out her hand to accept the gift, only to find that it was a red balloon - with

HAPPY BIRTHDAY printed on it. I don't know whether she posted the balloon to her granddaughter or whether she kept it, to hand it to her one day while telling her the story of how she found it.

Truly the world is far more miraculous than we can understand, and such experiences show that we can indeed communicate with and through the natural world. In the end, the deciding factor becomes belief: as the poet Aidan Dun says "Nothing here is real without belief". The psychologist Wayne Dyer echoes this when he says "You'll see it when you believe it", summarising decades of research by psychologists that show the primacy of conceptions, beliefs, in the perceptual process.

Maybe to see fairies we have to believe in them first.

Philip Carr-Gomm
Aotearoa - The Land of
the Long White Cloud
August 2000

Contents

Prologue		3
Chapter 1	A Faerie's Child	7
Chapter 2	Between Worlds	15
Chapter 3	Changes	21
Chapter 4	The Lifting of the Veil	35
Chapter 5	Growth	47
Chapter 6	Coming Into Focus	71
Chapter 7	The Faerie in the Jar	79
Chapter 8	Of Plants and Flowers	87
Chapter 9	Born From Flowers	95
Chapter 10	Flower Power	107
Chapter 11	The Lifting of the Spell	121
Epilogue		125
Appendix		127

Prologue

It was never my intention to become psychic. I knew
that there was a tradition in my mother's family of seeing
and hearing spirits, that my grandmother was "fey," that
two of my cousins had seen and talked with the ghosts of
people they had loved. Another cousin had seen "little
people" around her home, who had laughed at her. I had
seen faerie, elves and pixies when I was a small child, and
I'd been terrified by ghosts and dark presences that appeared to me in the night. Fantasy companions were more
real to me than my school friends well into my teens. That's
common in childhood, and I grew out of it as most children do, seldom giving the spirit world a thought after the
age of nine or ten.

During the 1980s all that changed. I moved back to the
country, where I belong, and at once the spirits of the land
took command of me. Every tree, bush and rock was alive
and speaking, and among them moved the Aborigine ghosts
and spirit people, who helped me to develop my psychic

senses. I began to remember those childhood encounters more clearly. There were the Aborigine spirit people who used to call me out of my body, while I was asleep and dreaming, to play as a spirit child with their children in their world:"Come on, little white girl, we won't hurt you!" There were the wild, laughing playmates I had, and two boys in particular: Peter, with his American accent, and Davy, with his tousled hair and handsome blue eyes, who was later to become my spiritual husband and the father of my ethereal children. I remembered the ghosts who showed me how they passed through walls, and the pictures and toys I had that became animated and talked to me. Even after these memories began, I was completely unprepared for what was to follow. First I started seeing faces in the mirror that were not my own. Monstrous or comical at first, they gave way to a succession of faces of animals, angels, fauns, faeries, devils, demons and more, all of which were visible to other people as well as myself. Soon, ghosts, angels, beings from beyond Earth, and a variety of other non-material beings were appearing to me. During almost a decade of intense psychic activity, four years of which I was bedridden in a small caravan, with only my mirror and two angels for company while this bewildering array of beings came and went, I was shown this amazing planet of ours from her insides out, given glimpses of her many dimensions and shown how she operates as a living being within her celestial environment. I was shown scenes from her past, present and future, and taken to vantage points outside the dimension of linear time to where I could get a sense of all three at a glance. The experience was wonderful, but it left me shattered. My personality had been taken apart and put back together again, leaving me telepathic, second-sighted, clair-audient —and, mercifully, still sane. It's taken me almost another decade to integrate all of these experiences to the point where I can begin to write some of them down. More than one mystic has warned that if you bring forth that which is within you, it will save you, but if you do not bring forth that which is within you, it will kill you. Mine is a story that needs to be told. But how? Where to begin? Looking back, those ten years were a tightly woven tapestry of many strands of experience. Remembering is a matter of sorting out the threads. Some strands are brighter, clearer, easier to follow than others, so it makes sense to start with them. Perhaps the clearest of all was the series of conversations I had with the faeries, first during my childhood, and then again as an adult, into the present day. It seems logical to start with them. . . .

Chapter 1
A Faerie's Child

I'm six years old, still weak and a little woozy from a bout of pneumonia. I fast naturally through loss of appetite. I am alone for long hours of the day, and I seek in my mind the perennial fantasy, the one that's always just there behind the finest of veils, calling me with a sweetness like dew drops. Taste one - it was that sweetness of being, that enchantment. Hyacinth, Violet, Hollyhock, and Iris are their names. They whisper, but I can't make out what they're saying. I'm neither in my hot, uncomfortable bed, nor am I quite in the English-looking meadow they are carrying me to in fantasy. The sky is silver-blue, yet my white plaster ceiling is there too. My breath is shallow, as much to avoid being too windy for these delicate beings as from the tenderness remaining in my lungs. "Are there boy faeries?" I whisper. I hear "yes," and "no," and more yeses and more nos. Images of pixies in caps, mysterious elves in snail-shell helmets, brownies, goblins, and others vie for a place in my vision. They drown out the faeries' answers, they break the spell, the meadow is gone from view, and I doze off.

Some thirty years later, bedridden with a different illness, shimmering again between one reality and another, I find myself again with a faerie almost visible by my hand, another near my mirror, and more among the plants in my bedside indoor garden. I breathe like a frightened child, shallowly, and I whisper so as not to make a faerie-bruising din with my voice, exhaling as gently as I can. Lisping, so as not to hurt them with the sharpness of my speech, I ask "Are there boy faerieth too?"

Faeries were my closest companions from about the age of three. I learned about them from picture books, stories, nursery rhymes, and songs, from my mother who often told me about them although she didn't believe in them, and from my grandmother who was fey. She could heal by touch and may actually have seen them. I spent my hours of play alone, deep in fantasy, talking in whispers with these wild little winged beings who lived among flowers, sipped dew and led me to do the same, and held dances in Faerieland or on the moon. They preferred midnight to any other time and mossy dells to any other venue. I tried to match my inner visions to the pictures in the books, to make my fantasy accord with them, and I asked about them endlessly.

"Have you ever seen one?" I would ask every older child or adult I met. Most would say no, but perhaps just to please me, some would say yes. My mother, who believed in encouraging children's daydreams, told me she'd often seen them when she was small, flying among the branches of trees. After that I searched every currajong tree that grew along the town's streets whenever we went for a walk. I searched in vain, but I sensed they were just beyond my vision, and if only I knew how to look, I would see them. My fascination grew. I looked for them everywhere: in the gardens in the town, in vacant lots and weedy lanes, even out in the scrub. Unlikely country it was, with its dusty mallees – sparse, stunted eucalypts, their limbs like arms with thin-fingered hands clutching dry, rattling streamers of bark. There were huge clumps of spiky spinifex and broad expanses of red desert sand between them, marked with the tracks of goannas and venomous snakes, fierce-eyed emus as tall as a man, and big kangaroos. The harsh cries of cockatoos and the incessant cawing of crows filled the hot blue sky: not a mossy dell in sight. So I returned to my fantasy, letting those filmy forms with rainbow wings and gossamer gowns who would not appear to my outer vision haunt my inner vision instead, which they did to the point of obsession.

"Here I am, on your shoulder," I'd imagine one saying. "See, I've got a green dress on. Look, I'm waving my wand. " Or, "Hold your hand out flat. Keep it still. Hyacinth is going to land on it. There. She's standing on your hand." And I would imagine that they really were there, that I really had seen, really had felt the touch of tiny feet on the skin of my palm.

As new information from books and stories honed my fantasy and sharpened up the detail, I started to "see" faeries everywhere. There they were in the stiff clumps of spinifex, dancing in the hidden patches of moss that grew in the hollows of rocks, flying with the down from the coarse desert thistles in the hot summer breezes. At dawn, they sipped the winy dew from gumleaves out of gumnut caps with appreciative sighs. If my imagination had run a little wild, it was not so wild as to lose touch with reality. On a subliminal level I knew the faeries well.

They fed my imagination in their own mysterious ways, keeping me in thrall, bringing me through the fantasy into direct communion with their realm. Sometimes the veil separating the fantasy from the reality grew very thin, and for brief moments it would vanish altogether. In gardens especially they drew me towards blooms, and kept me whispering my questions to them as I bent my face to the flowers, grasses and weeds. Not in every garden, though. Some instinct would tell me which ones had faeries, gardens made by people with that air some people have of a half-humorous, half-serious inner wisdom. When, at age five, I wanted to make a garden "for the faeries," these were the people who did not laugh, who instead gave me a pot of grape hyacinths, a head of hollyhock seed, a fistful of sweet william seedlings, or a runner of violets to plant.

The garden grew. I gave each flower, as it opened, a name, a personality, and a soul that flew to the faeries' dances at the midnight of every full moon. It was a sophisticated idea for a small child, and in retrospect I know it was beyond my imaginative powers. That separating veil is like an osmotic membrane: some elements pass readily from one side to the other under the control of the co-operating minds of the faerie and the child's higher self. My play was being directed to enhance my relationship with the faerie. In hidden places among my flowers I built "faerie rings," pressing moss into the soil for the faeries to dance on, edging them with pebbles or shells and strewing petals about. There were secret places: natural crevices in stones and hollows in logs, or little caverns eroded out of old, crumbling stonework in which I would leave gifts, notes, and tokens for them.

I once asked my mother, "If I leave hair ribbons out for the faeries at night will they wear them?" She assured me they would, but that they'd always put them back afterwards exactly as they found them. Faeries, she told me, are always neat and tidy.

Faerie morality was always an uncomfortable issue with me. I was not tidy, nor was I good. I was a temperamental tantrum-thrower. The faeries told me, perhaps humorously, that anyone else as bad as I was would not have faeries for friends, but that I was different. Forces beyond my control were making me bad tempered. This was not given in words but I grasped the idea, though with difficulty, because it puzzled me.

It still does, sometimes, although I've had insights into it since then. I paid a price for faerie friendships. I gained sensitivities and experiences that few children have, but lost some vital social instincts and the robust psychic self-defence system that most children take for granted. I suffered a lot of psychic harassment, (and still do), which often triggered my tantrums. Perhaps you almost have to be a faerie to commune with them – and faeries are temperamental tantrum throwers!

As I reached school age, faeries were practically my only friends. On the surface I appeared normal, if a little withdrawn. The faerie experience is alienating, however, and I was a severely alienated child. This wasn't evident to my parents. I played with other children at school, but I was uncomfortable with them and they with me. All my conversation was about faeries. I boasted of my intimacy with them though I believed myself a liar, as indeed sometimes I was. I found other children's conversations about their families and friends utterly bemusing.

Once, while stamping my foot in anger over some small thing, I bit my tongue and it hurt. "Wicked faerie!"laughed my mother. There was a wicked faerie who punished naughty children, she explained. I was six years old by then, and at the peak of my childhood powers as a seer. I asked the faerie about the wicked faerie, and was shown her. I was given a glimpse of a kind of metaphorical landscape. Human and inhuman interests and attitudes were represented as visible tensions, currents, pressures, and fluxes. I saw fields of overlapping influences, with busy interfaces between them. Excluded from it, but haunting its edges, was the wicked faerie, cold, glassy, brittle, and cruel. Shut out of the action by the common will, she nevertheless is bound to it, because every faerie is her next of kin. She's in pain, struggling against her bonds, half-crazed with fear and rage. She is stretched out painfully like one crucified, like the proverbial faerie caught in a web, at the extremities of these networks of power and access that humans and faerie weave between our species and theirs. She peppers us with curses.

It was a frightening vision, eerie, but I was not able to be afraid. The faeries would not permit it. They explained to me that there was a war being fought, and that I would be protected. In time, faeries and their allies would vanquish her.

I believed then, and continued to believe for almost another thirty years, that this clear, persistent memory was a child's fantasy. Now I can see how real it was, and how accurately I perceived the display.

Meanwhile I tended my garden, made my tiny fanes and shrines and daydreamed constantly about faeries. I drew pictures of them, made tiny faerie dolls out of wisps of fabric, and at night in bed when the lights were out I stayed awake for as long as I could whispering far into the night with these wild and wise, human yet inhuman beings, while that veil between the worlds grew constantly thinner.

Night after night I fell asleep with the faeries' voices zinging round my ears like a breeze through the spinifex: "You are our child, our child. You are our child. . . . "

Chapter 2

Between Worlds

"Our child," they said, and if that seems possessive there was good reason for it. I have learned that there are many beings that vie for access to psychically sensitive children. Moreover, faerie story writers depict a faerie land in which pixies, elves, gnomes, brownies, goblins, and others all live together. Any child who experiences faeries naturally wants to know about all these others. Elves intrigued me: "Are they the boy faeries?" I wanted to know. "Do they marry faeries? Can elves fly?" I got no answers from the faeries though I was very demanding, asking again and again, "Have they got feelers? Do they like dancing?"

The faeries kept me on a tight rein, but I had to know. In dreams and in play I felt out pixies, gnomes, brownies and elves, and satisfied myself that they were real and reachable. But the faeries maintained their enchantment and I soon returned to them, delighting in them more than ever.

In 1960, when I was eight years old, my parents suddenly moved us to another small country town on the south coast of Australia. It was a well-watered sheep farming and grain growing area. The native scrub had been almost completely destroyed and foreign fauna and flora were rapidly replacing it. In grassy meadows grew introduced wild flowers. Oxalis, scarlet camomile, poppies and black-eyed Susans, pink and blue statice, iceweed, and mallows bloomed among sparse native grasses where once there'd been dense scrub. In groves of imported pines grew exotic toadstools as big and soft as sponge cakes. These were hectic yellow underneath, slimy grey-brown on top, and exuded a pungent, poisonous smell. They looked big enough and magical enough to house the story book faeries of my infancy. I was utterly charmed.

The people there were of Cornish ancestry, the descendants of miners who had come a century before to mine copper. A fey and introverted people, their cottage gardens were full of faeries, as were the woodlands and meadows surrounding them.

My parents gave me plenty of freedom. With my pet cat for company I roamed the district looking for faeries. I'd learned by then not to whisper or talk out loud with them, to communicate by thought instead. The clarity and sureness of my awareness of them was fading, and I was lapsing more and more into pure fantasy. Glimpses of faerie reality were becoming rare.

Nevertheless, strange things happened. Once, I read in a storybook about a little girl who, having put on a faerie costume for a fancy dress parade, was late for the judging and had to run. She ran so fast "her feet scarcely seemed to touch the ground.." I gave this idea serious thought: it would be like flying, like being a faerie. I decided to try it. Holding an imaginary wand and flexing imaginary wings, I took off. Keeping an easy, springy tension in my legs, willing my toes not to touch the ground, reaching with my whole being for the air above, I sprinted. Toes pointed, knees high, I went up past the school garden, along the crumbling old greenstone wall, down along the row of Norfolk Island pines, back through the paddock full of fathen and mallow to home. This was a distance of about half a mile, and I didn't stop until I'd crossed our lawn and reached the house, in full view of my brother Graham.

The expression on his face took me by surprise. He looked not just astounded, but actually afraid, as if he'd just seen a ghost. That gave me pause, and I looked back on what I'd done. Certainly it was faster than I'd ever run before, and I was the second fastest eight year old in school. My feet had seemed to me not to touch the ground, only scudding a toe-tip over it every fourth or fifth step.

Only in retrospect was I able to gasp how strange that sprint had been. My legs had felt light and fleshless; I'd been moving by pure will. I'd been in a profoundly altered state of consciousness, seeing into another world as I ran, a world of low hills and valleys through which I had run for miles, far further than I'd run in this world. Yet I was seeing this world too, its familiarity looking stranger than the unknown world I was also in. I saw our world

17

through the eyes of an other-worldly being. It was all haze, glimmer and dazzle. The densest objects—walls, stones, the house—seemed to be made of thin cloud, while trees were webs of mist, and my brother was an elongated wraith.

I had landed laughing and light-headed, not a bit out of breath. Neither of us said very much about it. I don't remember being frightened myself, but, all the same, I let the incident slip from my memory rather fast, only recalling it on rare occasions as I grew older. I never tried anything like that again—at least, not until I grew up. I continued to roam about the countryside alone.

I often felt the faeries near me, especially in the early morning before anybody else was awake. I would kneel among the nasturtiums for a long time without moving, gazing into dewdrops. The air around me was so charged with that energy it has, just after first light and before sunrise, that it almost seemed to sing. I had a sense that there were many faeries there, almost visible as small disturbances in the light: glimmers and sudden flashes. I would stare into a dewdrop and become entranced. I was seeing with extraordinary clarity, responding not just to the power of beauty, but to a special quality that belonged to the dewdrops themselves.

Dewdrops have power, just as crystals, gems, and pearls do, but more, much more! Infused with the inner radiance of a single dewdrop, I would become charged with that radiance, and the effect would sometimes last all day. It lifted me up, made me light-footed and inclined to dance, and I could not keep from singing. It was the thinnest, highest, purest of silvery tones I tried for. From inside my head it sounded wonderful, and my cat enjoyed it too, but to my brothers it was an awful, eerie squealing, and my mother told me to stop it. She said it would strain my vocal chords.

Undeterred, I would go out into the bush and sing there. I sang myself silvery, until I felt crystal clear and as full of colours, reflecting and refracting within and about me, as a dewdrop. I would turn my face up to the sky, drinking sky-power just as the dewdrops themselves do. I felt at those moments as if I had no form, no weight, no location, but had become a being of pure spirit.

The faeries have since explained to me what I did not understand then: that while I was "drinking" the spiritually potent radiances of the dewdrop, the dewdrop was simultaneously registering the colours and shapes of my being. Every faerie or other being who "drinks" a dewdrop in this way makes a spiritual contribution to the essential nature of dew, affecting the "all-dew" (deva) through a single drop.

These experiences had not taught me to connect socially with the children I met at school, and I was beginning to enjoy the idea of myself as a "cat who walks by herself." I had a few friends, but my strangeness put a strain on friendship. They had faded to almost nothing when, after two years, my family moved again.

Chapter 3
Changes

The faeries left me alone for nearly twenty-five years. Adelaide was my new home, and as I entered my teens, the sixties were just beginning to swing. As always, my social life was sparse except for a couple of brief, close friendships, while my inner life was rich. By the end of the decade I'd discovered poetry, protest, and the peace movement, experimented with psychedelic drugs, dropped out of university, and left my parents' home. I worked for a while, read a lot, did without radio and television, as I still do, kept cats, and gardened organically.

But my world wasn't working. My psychic faculties were chafing under the veneer of so-called rationalism our culture tends to impose. I began to converse silently in my head with others, and after a while I became aware that it wasn't just my own crazy fantasy: at least some of them were really there. I could feel the pull of their minds on my train of thought, influencing its direction and altering its very nature. I was being helped to insights about myself, and life in general, that were otherwise beyond my experience. Within me, my dreams and subconscious experiences were threatening to erupt into consciousness. This was a major challenge to my belief system. I started seeing a psychiatrist, but switched to a life enhancing therapy known as Primal Therapy. Soon, I moved to the mountains of northern New South Wales with other "primalling" people.

They'd almost taken over a small village, and since no houses were available I lived in a tent beside a mountain stream all through one cold, windy winter, with a campfire for warmth and a hurricane lamp for light. It was a place of stunning beauty: steep, rain-forested mountains threaded through with small, fast streams. These had cascades and waterfalls, and their banks were overgrown with tree ferns, bracken and maidenhair ferns. Noisy black cockatoos heralded storms, cows and dogs roamed free, possums chittered around the campfire at night, and ticks and leeches found their way inside my clothing to drink my blood.

Despite occasional discomfort I loved it, and was on the point of buying land there. Then, one day, as I stood gazing at the flow of water over the pebbles of the stream bed, I fell into a deep reverie. I was conscious of beings around me. I could almost hear their voices, or rather feel the texture and flow of their voices as they talked, without actually hearing the sounds. Then one of the strangest, most moving experiences of my life came upon me: I felt, powerfully, the presence of the mallee: not merely the tree, although I had a clear vision of a stretch of mallee scrub, but of the formless, yet mindful, spirit of the land where the mallee tree is the dominant species. It was calling to me. There were no words, but it was articulate. There was pain, longing, love so deep it bewildered me, so personal it left me in shock. And it was calling, seizing me and carrying me off, home. It left no room for questions like "Why me?" and "What am I to you?" though they were whirling about in my head, unanswered. I wasn't even able to ask who or what it was. I just knew. I couldn't choose not to go.

Within a few months I had sold everything I owned and moved to an eighty-acre patch of scrub in the South Australian mallee, without power, water, fences, or any kind of dwelling, but an abundance of native wildlife. The day I first stood on that piece of land, a feeling almost as intense as the first took hold of me, of joy, of triumph, and of gladness. The piece of mallee was a subdivision of an old sheep farm. Most of the neighbouring subdivisions had been bought up as investments or weekenders and were seldom visited. They backed onto a large nature reserve unknown to tourists. I had a couple of square miles of wilderness practically to myself. It wasn't long before I began to feel the trees and bushes responding to me, and noticed the glimmers of beings here and there in the air, caught the first whispers of telepathy.

Three people came with me, but only one, Helen, stayed,

and is still here twenty years on. Within a year we had an old Jeep. Being close to the River Murray, we installed a pump on its banks and there was our water supply. We got some goats, some hens and a rooster, a cat, and somewhere along the line I'd acquired a scotch collie. There's no better breed of dog for a companion if you happen to be spiritually sensitive, because their mentality actively promotes psychic experience. We started on our gardens and orchard.

It truly was an enchantment. Every tree, twig and leaf was radiant with a light that was almost golden; certainly, it was visible. The trees, shrubs, and grasses surrounding our home for a radius of about a mile in all directions were visibly enhanced during that initial period, which lasted for about a year. It was so noticeable that you could see and feel a decline in the vibrancy and beauty of the vegetation, and even of the rocks and the earth, as you drove out of our space. The fade-out was so abrupt that it hit you just like a sudden change in temperature or in the quality of the air.

We were tangibly in connection with spirits of the land, even though the faeries had not yet announced themselves. No one visited us for weeks on end. The few who did, often commented upon the atmosphere, or else were visibly awed or made uneasy by it. They talked about the healing energy, the deeply peaceful, happy feel of the place, the vitality they felt during, and for some days after, their visit. One or two of our visitors felt friendly presences around us, and one visitor actually saw one of the presences that I'd been seeing.

Helen was as susceptible as I was to the mallee's enchantment. For her it was a timeless period of days that seemed to have no beginning and no end, of forever evenings, of starry nights full of living spirits. Stars, clouds, the sky itself, all vibrant with meanings that seemed so close to being grasped. She loved to be out in the mallee, finding dongas or rocky outcrops to stand on, where her sensitivity to the subtle magic of the plants and animals and birds was enhanced. She was feeling her way closer to the spirituality of the Aborigines who had lived here not so long ago.

Helen found a job in a nearby town, and went about the repetitive tasks of those days with the calm meditation of a priest performing her round of rituals in some ancient temple: getting wood, preparing food, managing our water supply, and caring for our animals and garden—and me.

While everyone else was being energized and vitalized, I was being deliberately weakened by the friendly presences who infused the place with its healing atmosphere. I know now that I was being made more attuned to them, more honed to their presence—not, this time, as an accepting child, but as a fully cognizant adult. The process was exhilarating, educating, and harrowing.

Very soon after we arrived I kept finding myself in front of the mirror, as if drawn there against my will. I've never been vain, so I felt uneasy about it, but soon I began to see not my face but a succession of other faces appearing in it. These included many different kinds of beings, all anxious to be seen and heard. As well as these, other beings were appearing to me as I went about my daily life, and among these were faeries. Most of the communication between us happened through sight, sound and touch, but more often other senses came into play that told me just as much. I would feel the energies of unearthly nearby bodies, the flicker and flow of their emotions, the qualities of being that make up their character.

By wordless telepathy I could communicate more information, a truer account of thoughts and feelings, more eloquently than words allow. Instead of catching a glimmer of light or a wreath of mist that was gone in an instant, I learned to hold a photo-clear image of whatever being I was communing with in my mirror for whole seconds, and sometimes minutes, at a time. I was able to show them to Helen and one or two friends, who, to my surprise, reacted with fear. Some we never saw again. It was fun, fascinating and frightening, sometimes terrifying.

In the mirror, I found our planet's invisible soul plunged into a savage and pathetic, psychical and spiritual war. My own self, being newly noticeable in the psychic and spiritual worlds, was under heavy attack, as I still often am. It has taken me a long time to realize that I was being attacked. I was often injured, weakened, and tormented in my subtle being because I did not know how to defend myself, or even that I should. I soon became so badly disoriented that I couldn't follow a train of thought. Finally I quite literally lay down and went to sleep.

For almost a month I hung between our world and theirs in a state of irresistible torpidity, opening my eyes only for a few moments every several hours. While in that state I was given visions, and was talked to audibly. Most of what they said I forgot, as soon as I heard it, but I was aware they were "operating" on my mind, adjusting my senses and organizing the flow of consciousness between them and my conscious mind, and vice versa.

Helen and I both knew that this was no ordinary illness; it was one that a conventional doctor would be powerless against. Symptoms came and went. Sometimes I would awaken abruptly out of my torpor and stand up, seized by a tireless energy that took me on long rambling walks through the scrub. I prowled through that wilderness of twisted trees and dense, spiky bushes. There, great crumbling slabs of lichenous limestone resounded to the cries of crows, ravens and cockatoos, while emus stared and eagles wheeled overhead, scanning the land with their all-seeing eyes, and kangaroos would go bounding away in the shimmering heat. More than the mammals and birds, however, it was the reptiles who possessed this land: goannas, bearded dragons, and sleek brown snakes, and the constant flicker and flash of skinks and geckoes.

All of these "spoke" to me. How I heard them I scarcely know, but they were eloquent. With my flagon of water in my hand, and supplies of dried fruit and nuts, I would walk from one place to another, feeling the power of the land, awakening to the teeming spiritual presences that haunt every tree and stone, till my head would reel with it. Then I would sink down into the cool sand in the shade of some gnarled old mother tree and lose consciousness—it was not normal sleep—for an hour, or two, or three, until "they" would pull me back to awareness again.

Setting off at daybreak, I'd return home at sunset and fall into bed exhausted. After a few days I'd go back into that deep, deep torpor, to listen again to the voices saying things I could clearly hear, but could scarcely believe. They were modifying my brain. They were undoing habits of thought and attitude, patterns of conditioned behaviour and response, and would help me to evolve new ones. I was pleased enough with this idea, because as I've said, the ones I had weren't working for me. It's also true, however, that I wasn't free to opt out, and my resistance, which sometimes expressed itself as screaming headaches, excruciating muscle cramps, and various levels of muscular pain, was simply being overruled. I was not just a helpless victim, they insisted. I had incarnated for this specific purpose, to be opened up and made to see some of this planet's extra-material dimensions.

"We are reducing the fear," they explained, but I wasn't aware of the fear then, although sometimes between periods of torpor I experienced episodes of trembling, as if with fear, and I tended to huddle up to the campfire for comfort even when the weather was warm. They had switched off my emotions, partly as a matter of mercy and partly so that fear and anger would not get in the way of good communication. I found it rather interesting to be able to observe my bodily symptoms of fear without actually feeling afraid.

Helen gave herself up entirely to these presences and never doubted the rightness of doing so. Every so often, upon emerging from my torpor, I would hear a voice using my throat to tell Helen what medication or food to prepare for me now, or when to run my bath. Most of the time, however, she was thrown on her own resources. She pored over books on healing and learned massage, acupressure, herbalism, and a range of other healing systems. She seemed to know, by an almost miraculous instinct or the instruction of the presences, how to help me: when to stand by me like a kind of sheltering umbrella; when to fight with me; when to humour me; and the best ways to care for me and ease my pain, whether with herbs or music, massage or talk.

Sometimes when I was beginning to recover, I would look at her and see her transformed, her face aglow and mirthful, talking comical nonsense, and making us both laugh. Very often she was wearing the faces I'd seen coming out of my mirror, or appearing from the darkness of my retreat.

As unusual as things were, our faith held out. As the enchantment gradually lifted—or we withdrew from it, or both—the backlash was traumatic. We'd been kept artifi-

29

cially cheerful, anaesthetized, and our fears repressed. Now these rushed in upon us, and we both reacted by having a series of terrible fights that ignited over nothing and resolved nothing, but were nevertheless cathartic and cleansing.

Helen's fear manifested itself as frequent, brief, but intense fits of crying and trembling. With clenched fists and eyes shut tight she would rock like a child and moan. Then she'd get up, yell rude remarks to the presences, whose ghostly forms she too could see and feel, and occasionally hear, and get on with life. "We love you," they told her. "Love, love, love." Somehow, she always had the strength and the presence of mind to do the shopping, cut the wood, and do the chores.

My fear manifested itself as moments of wild panic, as I tried frantically, by an effort of sheer will, to climb off this planet and into the arms of my "captors," hardly understanding what impulse had possession of me. I cried and trembled too, and sang every song I knew over and over again until they told me to stop. Then I, too, would yell at them. They were destroying my mind, dismantling it, pulling it apart. My habits of thought and attitude, my socially conditioned behaviour, what were they if not myself, who I was?

They talked of mutations, telling me I'd never be the same again. How dared they, I asked, terrify me like that? Who were they, anyway? I think they tried to tell me then, but I was too crazy with fear to understand.

I stopped going outside. Being inside comforted some deep-seated instinct to be under cover, even though it gave me no protection from the presences. Being inside became physically necessary also: as my courage failed, so did my strength, and I became weaker than ever, unable to stand up for more than a minute or two. Yet through all this, on some level of my being, I did know these presences, and I longed for my fear to subside so that I could let myself know them consciously. Despite the fear, I loved them.

Helen fenced off a small area close to my caravan for me, and I found protection there. In it I planted a tiny garden of a few plants. Though I could not stand up for more than a few moments at a time, I spent much of my day finding myself in the soothing company of plants. Accompanying them, again, came the faeries. Their arrival this time was immediately a steadying focus, a refreshment, still and clear and quiet.

At first I saw them only as indistinct shimmers among the plants, and then later as concentrations of misty colour. In this form I saw them enter flowers by flowing into them, and emerging from them too. My telepathy was improving, and although I seldom heard their words, never more than the insect buzz of a word or two zinging past my ear, I could receive their nonverbal thought-forms easily. They told me they were transferring energy loads from over-energized plants to under-energized ones. They explained that they could transfer the energetic equivalents of minerals and other nutrients from areas of surplus to areas of lack, thus enabling plants to thrive despite minor deficiencies.

These faeries were no longer communicating with me through fantasy, but directly into my conscious understanding, and they were less inclined to project fantasy images of themselves to me. These telepathic encounters were brief, only a second or so, but their communication spun out in my mind into a train of thought hours, days, or even years long. I can't remember all that they said, but the topics ranged from details of this alchemy and similar alchemical exchanges between planets, between stars, and between galaxies, mediated by celestial beings in just the same way, to an account of the way plants sometimes enlist the faeries' help to achieve long term evolutionary aims. For example: rosemary, they told me, is gearing up to achieve a thin frosting of silver over her leaves, both for its beauty and for the medicinal value.

I began to see the faeries more clearly. At first, I would see several at a time, in flight, and then just one standing a little distance away, then closer and still closer—always just for an instant—before it would vanish. Other things had changed, in addition to my "sight". I no longer had the sense I used to have of being an indulged child, befriended by the faeries because I was "special". Now, I was aware that the relationship was important. Faeries, and all the other beings I'd been seeing, are real, and the veils between their worlds and ours are getting very thin. If they aren't "birthed" gently and with understanding into our world now, the pressure will build and they will erupt violently into our consciousness at great cost to our sanity and theirs. People who are seeing them must give as honest and complete an account of what they see as they can, to anyone who seems likely to give it intelligent and open minded attention. Not only does this pave the way for a further thinning of the veil, but it will also turn some people's attention to their own psychic perceptions, and help them to focus on the faeries in their own lives so that they may improve their rapport until the communion becomes conscious for them, too.

That wasn't the only thing that took the sentimentality out of my attitude to the faeries. When the veneer of fantasy was peeled away and the reality began to emerge, I was shocked to see how alien they are. Although they are exquisite from a few feet away, with their rainbow auras,, close up they are often wrinkled and insectile, with large, almost bald, lumpy heads, and skinny, flat-chested little bodies. Their eyes are eerie. In fact, they are as alien as people from another planet, which is, after all, precisely what they are. They come from the moon.

Chapter 4
The Lifting of the Veil

A midnight in spring: overhead blazes the broad, starry river of our own galaxy. Behind me are the Southern Cross and the constellation of Orion. Almost at its zenith, the full moon shines, shedding beams less golden, less dazzling than those of the sun at noon, but not less powerful, penetrating or far-reaching. Tonight they seem preternaturally vital.

I'm squatting beside an extinct campfire, staring up at the moon. I've been brought outside: unable to sleep, jerked awake whenever I dozed, now I find myself here without a clue as to why. I shiver a little and I look up to the moon. From horizon to horizon every plant, stone, hill and hollow is silvered in the magnificent radiance. I'm struck by the fact that I can see the moonbeams falling like a fine, sparkling effervescence in the air. I can see them stream out of the moon, filling the air, falling over the land. I can even see them striking my bare arms. I feel a little afraid, but also eager. There's a music in that rain of moonlight: a strange sense of its being alive. Not just the moon, not just the Earth, the stars and the galaxy, but even the very beams they shed on each other are alive.

The moon stares back, mesmerizing me, gathering my attention to itself until it has it all. I become deeply entranced. After a while I feel very large, a giant, squatting on my haunches gazing down on the surface of the moon. It appears shrunken to the diameter of a hula-hoop, only a few feet below me. I can see every detail of its surface, its rocks and "seas" and the strange shadows that pattern its surface. Yet I'm still firmly on my little patch of ground next to yesterday's campfire. Then, suddenly, I'm small again, and the moon is as distant as before.

There's a difference now, in the way those magical beams are being distributed. They are still all around me, but they are no longer touching me, and there are none between the moon and me. Instead, there is a tunnel or tower of darkness, yet not darkness: this is latent, unmanifest light, like a concentration of some radiance even "brighter" than light though invisible,.

Down this tunnel the moon pours its power to me. It is a living, mindful energy, quite different from the casual silvery rain of light all around me, and it deepens my trance, taking possession of me. Rapt, unable to move a muscle, and in a state of profound calmness, I gaze into the face of the moon.

For a loaded moment all is poised, and then it happens: a faerie appears within that radiant shaft. She seems to be of that radiance, neither dark nor light yet both. She, or perhaps her spirit, or form, or the mathematics of her form, glides through that ray, seeming to be made anew moment by moment in a smooth continuity of being. So she travels towards me. She is no size, any size: the very notion of size is meaningless. She is transcending relativity. Distance, location itself, speed, all have lost their normal points of reference. The moon stays its "normal" distance away. It takes her only a few seconds to glide from it to Earth, and yet there is no sense of her having moved quickly.

A swift, yes, but a gentle glide, no faster than a bird in leisurely flight.

She is followed by another, then another, and another and another and another. I lose count. They flow at the rate of pulses in a vein for—how long? I don't know. A few minutes, half an hour, maybe more. My gaze is fixed on a part of the ray high above me, so I don't see what they do when they get close to me, or how they avoid colliding with me.

I don't sense them near me. Instead, I have a sense of their having dispersed while still high up in the air, with a movement like leaves scudding in a breeze, though the night is still.

I don't remember it coming to an end, either, but eventually I find myself staring up at an innocuous-looking silvery disc of a normally bland moon, shedding its radiance over the Earth in a perfectly ordinary fashion, and I'm pulled back to normal consciousness. What was that all about, I wonder. A migration? I ponder the timing: right in the middle of a significant alignment of the planets, still night, full moon, no cloud, Libra singing like a kettle in every atom of the Earth and the Moon, and through my very being. Tired out, I go back to bed and fall asleep.

I had to wait a few years for an explanation, and eventually it came from the faeries. The moon, as sentient a planet as Earth or Mars or any other planet (and a lot more sentient than most humans are), knew me from my childhood involvement with faeries, and had been seeking me. It had focused all of its awareness into that single, sensitive beam with which, like a weird kind of predatory being, it had captured and held me rapt.

Now, just as people have one or two or more so-called "subtle bodies" which are more or less complete in themselves, so planets have more than one body. In the case of planets, no one body is subtler or more substantial than any other. Our sensory organs tend to be attuned to what we call "visible matter" and are almost entirely insensitive to the "subtle senses". Nevertheless, like people, planets have astral, aerial, and ethereal bodies, and more besides.

To understand the process we must now focus on the aerial sphere of the moon. Unlike its material sphere, the moon's aerial sphere has an embryonic biosphere, and it includes a large population of faeries. The aerial part of the spectrum of substances is the faeries' natal environment. A large number of these faeries are dancing in, and within, and above a ring. They glide, flow, weave about

38

and strike and hold attitudes. They seem ecstatic, yet they are acutely conscious of the geometrics of their own bodies and the patterns they form in relation to each other in the ring, like birds flying in formation. It is a three dimensional ballet, graceful, full of tension and power, beautiful.

Just as a dream-catcher is supposed to capture the spirit of a dream, so the web of the faerie dance captures and holds the moon's soul, what some would call its deva, and then the faeries form of it a lens to focus that sensitive ray which took such possession of me on Earth. Struck by the power of this ray, I gaze in wonder. Wonder is a powerful form of spiritual energy; the moon uses the energy of my amazement to vitalise and sensitise the communication link between us.

These same faeries now alter their dance slightly to form a kind of open chamber into which the migrating faeries dance, one at a time, and are danced into harmony with their destination: terrestrial Earth. This puts them seriously out of harmony with their native Aerial moon. This chamber, formed of gesturing faeries, is so energetically tuned as to function as a kind of airlock, isolating the dancing faeries from the moon's energy field while their dance attunes them to the Earth's. Repelled by their own planet, they become attracted to ours, as like attracts like. Then at last, through the shift of emphasis this causes, they begin that wonderful glide down the moonbeam that I witnessed that night.

In those days, as now, I often woke up an hour or two

before daylight, from strange, magical dreams, into a unique kind of awareness I've always associated with faeries. Even in a totally dark night with my eyes closed, I see a soft, hazy light in which visions come and go, and I hear soft voices explaining things to me, though I only intermittently catch a phrase or two.

At such times my sense of location becomes tenuous. One moment I'm aware of being in bed, my dog's head heavy on my feet, a cat or two on my pillow, the voices and the hazy light playing about my head. The next, I'm feeling the cold air, hearing the sounds, and seeing the sights of another location, and very frequently the things I see are far out of their normal proportions.

I see a tussocky patch of deep russet velvet, as big as a dinner plate, growing out of an expanse of wonderfully textured green, jewelled with large oil-glands and veined with delicate ribs. It turns out to be the spore case of a fern frond. Its fusty smell is still with me when I find myself back in bed.

Another time, I see the back of a rose petal, thick and fleshy, arching out of its calyx to half my height, and I'm conscious of the faerie beside me, her face quite close to mine, so that, in retrospect, I'm amazed at two things: one, that my face had been the same size as hers, and two, that to have seen the rose from that angle we both had to be hovering in the air!

Usually, I awaken from such experiences as if from a trance, still cold from the outside air, still able to smell and taste the scents and flavours of the other place, with its sights and sounds sharp and clear in my memory. It is utterly unlike waking out of a dream. There's only a sense of a second, or two, of "lost time" between one location and the other.

Occasionally I'm aware of the transition when I'm returning into my body. I've been looking at an autumn leaf, golden-bronze, its edges crisply scrolled, its detail greatly magnified—my hand, a tiny faerie's hand, scarcely spans the space between two of its veins.

I'm aware of the faerie next to me, urging me to "Stay aware!" She takes hold of my upper arm and gives it a shake, the way a friend would. She's like someone I'm fond of, generating a warmth and trust I seldom have with other people, though in reality, she isn't familiar to my conscious mind at all. Still, I'm not experiencing her as "strange" at this time, though I am carefully avoiding seeing her, blanking out her face when I turn her way so that I see only a white blur, though her hands are visible enough. She puts one of hers next to mine on the leaf. It is parchment white, much thinner than mine, with much longer fingers, but strong-looking. It conveys, with its quick, purposeful movement, a very human mixture of patience and urgency, such as teachers have when they're teaching something simple and obvious to someone who is learning painfully slowly. She pats the leaf. I hear her talking, emphasizing words, but I can't quite make them out. Then I blank out as usual, but she gives a yell and I'm back there, staring at the leaf.

Then, it happens. I move backward and upward at about the speed of a car accelerating from a standstill on a city street – quite fast and smooth – and I increase in size at the same rate. My eyes remain fixed on the leaf, of which, apparently in obedience to the faerie, I have kept hold, and I see the proportions between its size and my hand's return to normal. Having returned to my body in this way, and before switching from the psychic mode to the norm of earthly consciousness, I am aware of a long cone of clear light through greyish semi-darkness. It extends from my eyes to the place I've just left, which appears to be about fifty feet down, and yet only a few feet, as if perhaps it's fifty feet from one perspective, but only a few from the other. At the bottom of this cone I see the clear daytime brightness of the place I've just left, the leaves, the bare twigs, and the ground below in a circle about three or four feet wide. It becomes hazier as I look at it.

I let my focus shift from this to the leaf in my hand, and back.

Finally, after four or five seconds, it dims out, along with the leaf and the hand that held it. Then I make the sensory shift back to my normal senses, and am mildly surprised to find myself in bed, still with the dog's head heavy on my ankles and my old tabby cat purring in my ear. The leaf is gone, but there is still the faint impression of the crispness of its edges on the skin of my fingers.

In time, I dare say, I'll be able to look at their faces dur-

42

ing such episodes, without the laborious and lengthy buildup that has preceded the few sustained views of a faerie's face that I've had. It isn't that they're so very alien or at all ugly, it's to do with the inability to harmonize the different levels of energy radiating from our eyes and theirs. They mediate, through their eyes, energies that cause my eyes to bounce off theirs, making my head spin and causing an uncomfortable surge in my life-field. Human eyes tend to make them spin bodily as if caught in a gust of wind, or else our glance may zap them from their current energy level completely.

From episodes like this one I came to understand that the faeries were teaching me in a very systematic way to enter their dimension, enhancing my psychic abilities in the process. In return, I use those enhanced abilities to help them to access our dimension more easily, and make increasingly prolonged visits to the humanly visible part of the spectra of being. Meanwhile we were becoming immune to each other's alien energies.

My little garden was an important catalyst; as it grew, it brought me closer and closer to the faeries in it. I found myself in an almost constantly altered state of consciousness, in which the power of life in all things revealed itself to me as pure, unmoderated beauty. It's true we use value judgements, self-deceit, evasions, and denial to protect ourselves from the power of beauty, or truth, or love, whichever you wish to call it. There is a point in us all at the heart of our awareness where the three are indistinguishable. We fear the power of it.

The faeries gave me no warning, except this gradual increase in my awareness of beauty, as they worked subliminally on my mind and soul to liberate my senses from the tyranny of that unfelt fear. One morning I left my little garden and moved weakly out into the larger garden beyond, drawn by a call from a violet plant. Violets love me, and I love them, on a level of personal affection. I found a little perfumed flower hidden among the dark leaves, and I suppose I let it touch my heart.

I Instantly I went past the old, nostalgic affection to a purer love. It was sublime. For the briefest moment in time I was taken up in spirit to a point that was transcendent, to a single unified point of mystical awareness, the more potent for being inarticulate, where colour, perfume, texture, shape, location, and the physical, the spiritual, and the aesthetic were one. It was a flower of an experience and it closed like a flower almost at once. I gave a cry of alarm and clutched at the ground, sensing that I was gripped by a power that could carry me swiftly right out of my native reality, into a totally alien state of blissful being not much different from death. I was frightened. I saw that it was possible to die of the beauty of a violet. I remember crawling backwards rapidly. Helen came out and without any prompting, treated me for shock.

I stayed away from plants for a while after that. I'd been taking in a lot of information from the faeries and I needed time to integrate it all, to link some of this new knowledge I was acquiring to what I'd already learned from my education, my reading, and just by being alive. I needed contextualising information to help me make sense of experiences that could not easily be related to my ordinary knowledge of the world.

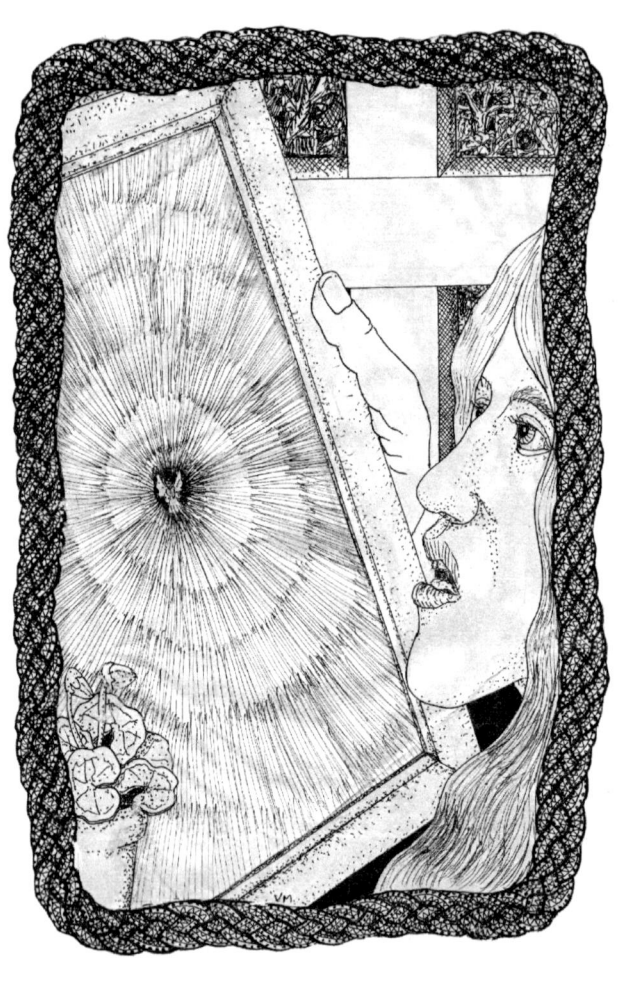

Chapter 5
Growth

By this time I was living my life as if the rest of the world didn't exist. I spent most of my time in or on my bed, in a tiny caravan full of plants, cats, an old wood stove, and my mirror. I cut pictures out of magazines, pasted them on my wall, and dove into their imaginative possibilities. "You are under an enchantment," I warned myself, but I loved this wild, weird world of the psyche, and could no more turn back than fly.

Fortunately, Helen was there, and occasionally friends would visit; I was aware that a "New Age" was burgeoning out in the world. Findhorn was making much of its faeries, and there were other accounts of them proliferating as well. Scotland's Findhorn, famous for its faeries, elementals and devas, is the home of the Findhorn Foundation, which is a well-respected centre of teaching about the various beings of the spirit world. These faeries didn't much re-semble mine, and neither did a host of beings that are or have been called faeries. These range from awarenesses without forms of their own to the magical giants of Norse and Celtic mythology, from plant spirits to malicious little imps.

I asked my moon faeries to explain themselves. Naively, I sat with a pen in my hand and an open exercise book on my knee, waiting for them to start. Nothing came. My anxiety increased. All these other witnesses to faerie couldn't be wrong. They either had the authority of myth, or they tended to agree with the Findhorn model. Was I then the victim of my elaborate, years-old delusion, and nothing more? This doubt was frightening, because my interconnected universe of "hallucination" now had absolute control of me.

I needed time to settle, time to build my abilities and my senses so that I could learn more. While my body remained weak, cloistered within the bounds of the caravan and the garden, dependent upon Helen, in time my subtle senses increased. I learned to master the fey, swoony enfeeblement that close and prolonged contact with the moon faeries had brought: transmuting it to a kind of wan, vaguely distracted detachment. This enhanced my psychic abilities, enabling me to bring the faeries down much nearer to the terrestrial plane, and to hear, but not yet participate, in their conversations. As I grew stronger, I could stay with them for much longer than the bare seconds that had thus far been my limit. I caught much witty banter, amidst the hampering effects of energetic incompatibilities, which instructed and entertained me.

Still, there were limits to how much and what kind of conversation I could understand.

They suggested much without actually telling me anything for certain, only adding elusive hints and rare glimpses to my tenuous fabric of data, setting my theories and guesses swirling. As delightful as it was to familiarise myself with them and with these modes of experiencing, it was still frustrating.

To complicate things still further, in my garden my vision had opened up to reveal all kinds of different beings: pixies, devas, nature spirits and elementals appeared, all connected with plants, and I had to learn (in fact I'm still learning) to distinguish all these from the moon faeries, who rather pointedly refer to themselves as "true faeries" —as if somehow the other sort either weren't "true" or else weren't faeries. In this way the moon faeries distinguished themselves from the Findhorn faerie types, perhaps in response to my questions about them.This removed much of my anxiety and my rapport with them improved dramatically.

I gradually pieced together the story of their evolution, which includes parts of the story of our own: although we started out as distinct species, it will come about that our two species will merge into one, far more diverse than both put together. This will be only one of many mergers made by both species with other species of human-like beings of other dimensions. In the case of the faeries, it's already started.

To contextualize: planets are life-forms, just as we are. Humans have specialized cells to perform their various functions of body and mind, and planets have organisms, both material and extra-dimensional, including humans, plants, animals, angels and so on, to perform their various functions.

Our cells' shapes and functions are determined by our genes. Our scientists haven't discovered it yet, but the faeries assert that a planet's entire array of life forms, both material and non-material, are determined by planetary "genetics," forces within the planet that regulate the evolution of its beings. A planet like Earth generates its angels and its biological life forms separately at first, until both are developed enough to unite. People are incarnate angels, for example. The moon's "angels" are the winged faeries, with insect-thin bodies and eerily magical eyes. They need the help of the Earth to create their material life-forms, and to manifest themselves as material beings on the Earth first, and eventually on the moon. At the same time, the faeries provide us with the means of evolving moon-worthy aerial forms of our own.

It began when the first faerie appeared to the first fey humans, in early paleolithic times. These first appearances sent a shock through our planet, and produced a succession of very specific mutations in both faeries and humans. We diversified, and some people made slight shifts in the direction of faerie evolution, becoming a little more like the faeries. They, in turn, made similar slight shifts in our direction. We tended to become thinner in proportion to our height, and they became a little broader, and more rounded. Our eyes are becoming larger and more elliptical, while theirs are becoming smaller and squarer. Our noses and mouths are becoming more diverse and, generally speaking, smaller, while theirs are getting larger. Our gestures are becoming more graceful and precise; theirs, more casual and less calculated. Our magic, though we're mostly not aware of it, is becoming less brutal and warlike, and theirs less fanciful and less controlling. Sexually, faeries are becoming less casual, while humans become more open to faerie bisexuality and less defined sexual relationships. Although these processes began in the far ancient past, it's still only just beginning, and will take thousands of years, perhaps a million years or so, to complete. This is our story so far, as they told it to me.

After a few thousand years of intense interaction with selected human cultures, usually through their shamans, faeries have adapted themselves towards us and we've adapted ourselves towards them, through ritual, magic and other means—cosmetic means, for example, from the kohl eyeliner of ancient Egypt to modern eye-enlarging and lengthening cosmetics. Faeries have now reached a point where selected souls can incarnate as the human children of carefully chosen human beings.

At first, the host families were fully acquiescent, and had undertaken much special ritual preparation to achieve it. Inevitably, though, the first babies born in this way were not quite human. Even in historical times, the "faeries' child" was frail, feeble, feeble-minded, and fey, with decidedly strange facial features and a very short life-span. Furthermore, they tended to hover between our world and the faeries' aerial world, mediating an ultimately terrifying magic into the human, material world that endangered both material structures and the aerial structures of the faerie realms. It was traumatic for both, but it made it possible for an aerial being to bring down her own understanding to the human level, and so there was a fertile intermingling of our two wisdoms at least at the subconscious level. It was a fraught encounter, and very intense.

Humans took fright, became hostile, and human-faerie relations have never been easy since. The moon-earth marriage is not one that can be called off, however, and neither can the process be put off. Over thousands of years, we grew better at accommodating each others' differences. These days, faeries are so well integrated into our gene-pool that only people who know them well can distinguish their incarnate souls from those of other incarnates. They tend to be physically slender, even gawky, and either very quiet, timid, and conventional, or wild, outrageously witty people.

They are often involved in the arts—in dance, drama and the media—and because they all began as female, but tend to opt for birth as males because that is how male moon faeries evolve, they are often very ambiguous about their sexuality. Their gestures, often described as "feminine," are not actually at all like those of human females, but like those of faeries. This type of male faerie returns to the aerial faerie realm, after having died in the human, to become sexually flexible, able to change from one sex to another at will.

Our culture, in order to receive these births, has shifted its genetic trend faerie-wards, to the extent to which human beings who are attracted to the faerie realms by their own ambition, or by the needs of our planet and the moon's, are able to approach it via those conceptions in human wombs that are close, and only just fail, to be able to accommodate faerie souls.

The child is then attended by faerie guardians (those faerie godmothers of fiction) throughout his or her life, and goes, after death, to the aerial faerie realm to "incarnate" as a faerie. These are probably as numerous as faerie-souled humans. Let us hope they are better treated by the faeries than their people are treated here by ours.

This brings us to the present. Of the future they gave me only disconnected glimpses. I saw, over the next few thousand years, human beings expanding the scope of their senses and developing new senses that would enable us easily to see and interact with a whole range of beings on the aerial planes, and with still others about whom we know almost nothing now beyond scraps of myth and fantasy. I saw many beings of many different dimensions and planes of existence learning to move their own bodies from one dimensional plane to another, and to project themselves out of their bodies into other worlds, or across space within this one, in whatever forms or sizes seemed fit.

To give an example: one might need to communicate with a faerie living on the moon's ethereal surface. One would project oneself, in a faerie form, to manifest instantly in the vicinity of the faerie friend.

Meanwhile, the local body would go on with life as normal while waiting for this "plenary expansion" to return with the results of the communication, which would then, perhaps in a dream, become known, along with the plenary expansion's fresh, vivid memories of the transaction.

Certain shamans and highly trained, or in some cases closely bred hereditary tribal magicians, are already able to perform these feats, but the faeries wanted me to understand that they're talking about the ordinary people of the distant future. They explained to me some aspects of the role of technology in this: "technology" now offers a safe analogy to us, a virtual reality within which we can experiment harmlessly, as a path towards this future of subtler technologies.

As they talk to me, our planet expands to many more than three dimensions, and its amazing cultural diversity begins to make sense.

Every "pauper child's yen" of a belief system, every tribal or national custom, becomes a thing of great meaning and value, with a role to contribute to the future.

There is more involved, then, than just the marriage of

the Earth and the moon: without this marriage, the faeries tell me, the Earth would be doomed to abort like an unfertilized egg. I am still not sure why, but I continue to learn.

I will return now to the story of my early lessons. While I was recovering, I was attempting to heal myself with herbs. As well as feebleness and out-of control psychic experience, I was suffering from a bewildering range of physiological symptoms, not all of which had obvious causes. I would focus on a particular symptom, go to the indicated plant, eat a leaf or a flower, and feel my body's response to it. The method was quite successful. Some herbs, such as sage, thyme and marjoram, I kept near me because I loved them, without quite knowing why. Sage in particular was a kind of spirit guide for me in the realms of plant spirits; it helped me to distinguish these from the moon faeries. It fine-tuned my psychic focus and lifted me to the level on which faeries operate, enabling me to perceive them far better than ever before. In fact, it sensitised me to a specific kind of permeating energy, like the Hindu concept of prana, which is associated with a preternatural clarity of mind, reduced emotion, and acute spiritual sensitivity. With sage, I learned to allow my own thoughts, restless attempts at reasoning, and irrelevant preoccupations to subside so that those of the faeries could reach my consciousness. As soon as I was lifted up high above the chatter and glare and noise of normal consciousness, I reached the aerial world, where I was able to perceive nature spirits, elementals, faeries of many kinds and other spirit beings as well as moon faeries, in greater clarity and more coherently than I ever could before.

Heady it was, and I was inclined to feel dizzy and to experience periods of vagueness, losing myself in reveries from which I would emerge without the least trace of memory of what I'd been thinking about, or rather perceiving, because often I had the tantalising feeling that I'd been seeing things marvellous to my mind. I tended to lose all sight and sense of the material world, which had faded, anyway, to a dim transparency. I found myself in the odd situation of listening in on conversations some other part of my mind was having with faeries, and apparently had been having for some time, though I can't now remember much of what they were about. I became more relaxed, lighter, almost less substantial, yet I felt reassured. My contact with the faeries was building, and it gave me the confidence and trust to let myself go further than I ever would otherwise have had the courage to do.

I found myself gifted with visions of the wonders of the earth, from the deepest deeps to the highest heights. I would stand in the middle of the clear space surrounding our campfire and feel raised or lowered great distances, just as if I were in an elevator, although I also kept a sense of my terrestrial surroundings. Going down, everything would begin to feel denser, darker, more full of latent power, heavy and magnetic. Going up, the atmosphere grew wan, then dewy, then shining and silvery, and then bright with a beautiful, numinous light. I paused once on the dewy and glistening level, the aerial plane, and confirmed that it was here I had been seeing faeries.

I met more faeries, and was entertained with histories of the effects faeries have had on the languages of the terrestrial world. As well as being buffeted by emotional energies, and by the sharp blasts and gale-force gusts of breath produced by human speech, the faeries are sometimes painfully sensitive to certain sounds, especially "s," "t," and "c" sounds. For their sakes, I learned, many people who are subconsciously close to faeries lisp. In Spain for instance, the population was converted to lisping en masse, ostensibly after the fashion inspired by a lisping king, but in reality out of consideration for faeries. The French language was also commended, for its soft consonants and for its tendency not to pronounce many, especially final, consonants and even whole syllables. Gaelic languages, too, tend not to pronounce many of the letters in words whose spelling indicates that they were once pronounced.

Still, I couldn't stay in the aerial realm long. After a short few minutes I would be overtaken by a sweet, swooning feeling. Drained of strength, I would drop to my hands and knees, and sometimes I'd be too weak to make it back to the caravan without help from Helen. My journeys left me in half-states, however, where Helen could sometimes not find me. Once, finding my caravan empty, she came towards me where I sat just outside the garden gate. She leaned over the gate and called me. I looked up at her, and seeing that she was looking straight at me from only a couple of yards away, I didn't make the effort, which tends to be considerable when I'm attuned to the Aerial plane, of finding my voice to answer her. I just waited. She looked at me, through me, past me and around me for several seconds. Then she turned and walked away, calling my name louder than before. I pulled myself back to earth and called her back. Utterly astounded, she declared that she had not seen the least trace of me.

One day I noticed that my lemon-scented verbena, a favourite of mine and a real faeries' plant, had begun to wilt. I stared at it in dismay wondering what could be wrong with it. Suddenly I heard a voice in the air saying, " 'Er wants 'er trystal." It was a female voice, speaking in an archaic English dialect from, I suppose, Tudor times, or thereabouts. Before I could react, I found myself staring at a vision of a handful of large white crystals which was forming before my eyes. I saw them gradually shrink to become almost lost among the individual crumbs of good garden soil. Then I understood that I was being told my soil lacked the crystalline component that good, loamy soils should have: tiny crystals of silicon dioxide that concentrate vital energies and re-radiate them at life-enhancing wavelengths beneficial to soil organisms and plants.

At the time I was so beguiled by the voice and vision that I could not even register surprise. "Oh yes," I said, as if a perfectly ordinary passer-by had given me this gardening tip. "I've got some of that." I sprinkled some coarse river sand, all aglitter with the right kind of "trystal," around my plant. Sure enough, it improved almost overnight, and continued to thrive better than it ever had before.

As the spell lifted I realized that I hadn't seen the speaker. Who was she? A faerie? It felt like one, but why would she be speaking to me in that archaic dialect? They had always spoken to me in almost accentless modern English before. The strangest thing was that she had left a peculiar spheroid pool of pale light next to the verbena bush, about two and half feet in diameter, like a stain that affected the colour of the soil and stones and small plants growing within it. Viewed through it, they appeared to have been first bleached, then washed over with the delicate tint of palest sky-blue.

The experience worried me. I avoided the pool of light for a few days, and then gradually forgot about it, letting my vision shift from that part of the spectrum until I could no longer see it.

Inevitably, as I tended the garden, I ended up kneeling in just that spot without realizing it.

First I fell into a trance, and was filled with that wan, bluish light. I could feel energy focalized around me, and moving in ways that pulled with a gentle, almost tidal suck and sway at my mind. I found myself peering into a dense aerial mist in which a shape was forming. Surely, my gaze was pulled into sharp focus, and I was staring at a tiny face with eyes that caught and held mine like two hypnotic wells of power. I was alarmed at first, but I soon began to relax and laughed, saying, "Of course, this is what it's all about!"

At that point I noticed she was holding up a long, exquisitely thin wand that appeared to be made of a kind of anti-light, though I scarcely know what I mean by that. It was paler even than the wan daylight of the aerial plane, like a slit in the substance of the very air she stood in. It was this wand that was creating the tidal pull I was feeling, but I hadn't seen it until she began to wave it from side to side, quite slowly, in a wide, sweeping movement. At that, an eerie wave of energy passed through me which almost erased my mind. I went deaf, blind, transparent: the world was nowhere.

This was anathema. I panicked, yelled a soundless thought-prayer to anyone who might hear me, and at last felt myself jolted, by a mind-wrenching shudder, out of the flow of the wand's power and that eerie sphere of light. I was tumbled ignominiously backward onto the path. I scrambled to my feet and fled.

Over the next few hours the sphere dissipated, but my fear took a little longer. Were they evil, these faeries? Why would they want to hurt me? Gradually, I came around, as I was laughed at and remonstrated with by the faeries. At last I conceded that I hadn't been hurt, and that, scared as I was on one level, on another I was fascinated, delighted, genuinely pleased to have been shown not just the sweet and pretty side of faeries, but the sinister aspect too. The faerie in the blue light had in effect answered an unasked question of mine that I hadn't known I'd wanted to ask: why are people so frightened of faeries? A glance at traditional folklore reveals that we harbour some intense anxieties, along with the delight and fascination, concerning these alien little beings. In the answering she'd given me a deliciously scary thrill.

The story is not yet finished: a few years later I came across an old belief that faeries will help gardeners with magic and advice, but they demand payment in the form of crystals which must be buried in the earth. Then I understood: my faerie had been trying to explain that belief to me, and since words weren't yet working, she'd used a kind of charade. She'd shown me the crystals in a faerie's hand first, and that had given me the impression that they were large crystals. It was the same vision she'd created for some Tudor-era English gardener, and he or she had made the same mistake. By showing me the same crystals, now dwarfed in a human hand, she'd corrected my initial misconception. She'd used that accent to refer me to the time and place of the earlier conversation, when the old belief had arisen, and then waved her wand at me to explain why this English gardener feared faeries enough to imagine that they'd need appeasing.

I'm a terrible gardener by most people's standards. I love weeds.

Perhaps the faeries taught me to when I was small. I've always planted irises and violets and jonquils in my gardens, but I also adore the jade green and muted crimson stripes along the stem of the sturdy fat-hens, and the pungent, scalloped edged leaves of its smaller, darker cousin of the same name.

I love nettles, clover, fumitory, thistles, spurge, oxalis, and the many kinds of grass that grow of their own accord wherever nature plants them. At that time I had only my tiny stretch of garden, and I had to harden my heart against most of its weeds, only letting them grow along the edges of the path. Mallows thrived there, with wild mustard and barley grass, and the occasional stinging nettle. Though some of these are greedy feeders, my plants grew the better for their being there—except one, my garlic. It was only one garlic plant, and there were plenty of others in the main garden which Helen was maintaining, but I was fond of it. I'd been feeling a strong rapport with its spirit and I felt it had been talking to me. At first, it had put up a brave, bright spear, but then it paled, went limp, and stopped growing. It wasn't just not thriving, something was killing it. It didn't seem to have any of the symptoms of disease or deficiency in gardening books, and I couldn't see anything eating it or infesting it in any way. I went inside to rest, but it preyed on my mind. What could be wrong? Was there anything I could give it, some way to heal it?

I was accustomed by then to the manipulation of my state of consciousness by other beings, and the manipulation of my thoughts. I was aware of a group of five or six faeries keeping themselves at the outer edges of my aura, holding me in a communion with them. As I dwelt on the garlic, I began to "see" images from these faeries. At first I thought that what they were showing me and telling me was a silly fantasy of my own, so I kept trying to suppress it so that I could hear them directly instead. The images continued, though, beyond my control, so I sat tight and let things happen.

The story was told by means of telepathy and a kind of wrap around, holographic, cartoon style of movie, with the soft colours of a children's picture book. There were occasional audible words and phases, repeated at times to emphasize key ideas:

There was a war between an octopus and a sea-turtle. The octopus was a large, soft, white but translucent, female thing, alive with a graceful manner and an eager, efficient power. She danced for a while, and then curled her tentacles up over her head till they met right on top, their tips curling outwards just a little like a crown.

As I watched, she became harder and denser, solidifying into a firm, white, many-ribbed bulb, with its little tentacle crown arranged neatly at the top. A further slight change, and little green spears emerged from the crown, which had shrunk to thin, papery points. The octopus had shapeshifted into a bulb of garlic and begun to grow. There she was in her bed of earth, putting out fleshy white roots like an array of new tentacles. I saw her release thousands of tiny "octopuses" into the soil "sea," from her roots. They seemed to be large proteins or proteinaceous substances, pheromones perhaps, and they swarmed outwards with the same eager efficiency that their mother had shown. Wherever they went, those plump, tentacle roots followed, for they seemed to be preparing the soil for her to follow. The garlic thrived.

Into my vision next entered the sea turtles. First, angling its flippers through the rocks and reefs of the virtual ocean which filled my caravan, was a giant sea turtle that seemed to have emerged from one of the pictures on my wall. I saw it loom above me like a great bird. A dozen little octopuses went scudding after it, like sparrows in pursuit of an eagle. The turtle banked in dismay, and paddled smoothly away to take refuge among the roots of a beautiful mallow plant, also in the sea of the soil solution which it shared with its neighbour, the garlic plant.

I saw the mallow caress his sea-turtles, millions of them, with his aura, giving them ripples of energies that stimulated and vitalized them. By now, they had only the basic sea-turtle body shape and were tiny transparent soil organisms. The mallow nourished them with a soupy composition carefully regulated by the mallow's own biochemical magic for the benefit of its little "turtles."

Keeping near their protector, I saw these tiny turtles going out to forage in drifts of thousands, foraging among the soil aggregates, the rocks and reefs of this soil "ocean," and returning home to excrete rich mineral wastes in among the root hairs, so that the mallow could feed on them even when the soil was dry. This, I thought, explains why it stays so green so long into the summer heat and parching drought of December, long after all other introduced weeds have died off.

Suddenly I saw great clouds of the garlic's tiny "octopuses" swarming at the edges of the mallow's root zone and attacking the turtles. They left them dead or dying, their bodies flaccid and leaking into the soil. I felt fear and consternation possess the whole of the turtle population, and felt also the mallow's rage. His blood was up. In defence of his tiny flocks, he reared himself up like a tiny man, not a faerie, whose feet and legs were formed among the roots of the plant and whose hands and head were in the leaves, with his body the stem. Incensed, he lifted both hands, and from his long wizard's fingers there crackled forth a deadly electrical current of power, aimed at the heart of the garlic bulb.

The mallow was "pointing the bone" at my garlic plant, singing it to death, killing it with something very like hatred. "Mallow hates garlic," echoed faerie voices from one part of the caravan to another. "Too octopussy. . . kills the sea-turtles. . . . "

I pulled out the mallows growing near my garlic, relegating them to the compost heap. While it is a wonderful herb, and I was learning to converse with it too, on another level, we had plenty of it. The garlic recovered slowly, but never amounted to much.

One day I wanted a load of compost for my garden, but Helen was using the wheelbarrow for another purpose.

I'd have to wait, or think of something else. I could hear the old iron barrow rattling and clanking heavily over the ground, its big iron wheel squealing cheerfully at every revolution, bucking and baulking at every stick and pebble in its path. I looked at my unmulched garden and wished we had a second wheelbarrow.

My mind strayed to the brightly coloured advertising leaflets from our local hardware shop, to the pictures of smartly painted, deep-trayed, pneumatic-tired, rubber-handled wheelbarrows, and I tried to remember how much they cost. Could we afford one? I decided we couldn't and began carting the compost over to the beds in a small bucket instead.

It was an insignificant incident and I thought no more about it. No doubt I would have forgotten it completely within a week or so.

Only two days later, however, Helen and I had driven in the Jeep to the back boarder of our property to get a load of wood, when suddenly we saw, under the trees beside our road and just within our boundary line, a wheelbarrow. It was big and green, with a good deep tray, a pneumatic tyre, and rubber handles. It was not brand new: its paint was chipped here and there and had lost its lustre, but it was solid and sound and beautiful.

It was empty, except for a few scraps of bark and a dead leaf or two, and there was no one around for miles. That was strange enough by itself, but as I stared at it the memory of my casual wish two days earlier flashed into my mind. I could not dismiss the idea that that wish was granted here. Helen and I tried to work out whose it could be or how it could have arrived there. There was no sign that anyone had been carrying anything in it. Sometimes people take old weathered stones, or bush soil for their gardens, or collect firewood from under the mallees, but nothing of that sort had been disturbed. There were no car wheel tracks or footprints that I could see, just its own, single tyre-track coming across open grassland from nowhere. It was a complete mystery.

We left it there for two days and no one came to claim it. At last, feeling only a little guilty, and with a consciousness of being laughed at by the faeries, I wheeled the thing home, and a very useful wheelbarrow it's been! I don't doubt that some human agency was involved in putting it there, but why would anyone wheel a perfectly healthy wheelbarrow out into the scrub and leave it there? Perhaps that's one more thing the faerie will explain to me as the telepathy between us improves.

Those were confused times. In spite of my improved psychic perception I was not always sure of distinguishing the moon faeries accurately from other small beings. While I had, and still have, good second sight from time to time, I usually got only short glimpses of most of my visitants, or saw then only as hazy outlines, vague shadows, or shiny shimmerinesses in the air. Once I tried to call a faerie into my mirror, thinking that I'd be able to hold her image there and so get a sharper picture than I'd yet had. I've never had the patience for the soft sighted, mild, meditative gazing technique I've read about since these intense times in the mid-eighties, and I'm glad now I'd never been taught it. My method, which is highly successful, is to stare hard, full into the mirror in a state of high excitement and expectation, as if you're seeking someone across a street and you really wanted them to come to you. Usually it isn't long before the reflection starts "scrolling" from one face to another and, at last, there comes the wonderful sense of staring through my mirror into someone else's room or landscape, or even into another world.

In this way I once called a faerie into my mirror. I was aware of her response to me as she came into harmony with the reflection, ready to appear there. To my horror, her image formed at her actual size, about six or seven inches tall, at a distance from the mirror in a kind of vortex, and I saw her expression change from one of nervous excitement to panic as she was suddenly pulled at great speed towards the mirror's surface. Then, as she touched the glass, she slipped away sideways and vanished. Was it a joke? I didn't think so at the time. I was aware of her companions—I've never known a faerie to appear without five or six companions—and they too seemed shocked. After a few moments of consternation they left. I've never understood what it was about, but it must have been all right since they were soon back. I didn't try the mirror experiment again!

Chapter 6
Coming Into Focus

As time passed, I would often see faeries in the garden and in the caravan among my plants. Silvery and transparent, they had wide wings and long, rather full dresses, with delicate, lacy patterns in the weave. Their movements were graceful and flowing. Nevertheless, when I tried to make a sketch of one to show to Helen, I realised how little detail I had. Trying to focus my eyes on the shimmer of a faerie beside a plant, I would find that the very act of looking would concentrate the normally diffuse energy my eyes give out into an intense beam that instantly blipped the faerie out of the visible, vibrational range, and she would disappear. I found myself having to ask, "What are your feelers like? How long? Tapering or clubbed like a butterfly's?" Frustration would follow at not being able to hear them.

I tried a few sketches, and the faeries did their best to help me. It was an inspired exercise: the right brain activity of sketching, feeling intuitively for the form and detail, disarmed me, broke down my left brain defences, and stopped me distressing the faeries with my constant efforts to see them. Furthermore, it took me back to my childhood when I had drawn faeries constantly, and restored to me that conversational mode that had worked so well for us then.

Conversation at last! Except that this time there was no intervening fantasy. I was aware of a broad band between us in which our ideas mingled, negotiated and formed a veritable "conversation," although still not verbal. While sketching, too, I was aware of being part of a long tradition of psychic artists, who sift their intuitive knowledge for the details of faerie faces, faerie attitudes, and faerie raiment, and have the answer gently ushered towards their consciousness by faeries. The faeries were patient, shuffling to the front of my mind memories of details from children's picture books, faerie art, and occasional rare projected images of the real thing. These filled the gaps in my sketches, and corrected errors. Gradually I gave the faeries more control of my pencil, letting them make a curve here, an angle there, a tilt to one line and an elongation to another. There emerged a convincing image of a faerie's face and wings: the large, tilted eyes, grainy striped iris, vertical elliptical pupils, clubbed feelers, deep wrinkles around the eyes and neck and the joints of their long, skinny legs, narrow chin, long ears, and wispy hair. Yet it was many years before I finally brought all these features together in a single sketch, held it up to look at it, and saw it flash with a sudden blaze of magical light, saw the true faerie who had helped me with it shining through, smiling a congratulatory smile so full of power and radiance it took my breath away.

Faerie magic is full of this kind of power and beauty, but the drains upon my physical and psychic being continued to be considerable. Besides, I was under a greater enchantment not of their making which forced me to do what I earnestly wished to do: to explore the psychic realms with all the senses I could muster, and to bring back to normal awareness as much information as I could about the beings I found there.

"Telepathic conquest," someone ethereal once called my enchantment, and conquest is precisely what it was, though I still do not know its cause. I would, for example, plan a trip with Helen to one of the nearby towns just to sit in the Jeep while she did the weekly shopping. I was already feeling so alienated and so altered by my experiences that the normal seemed strange and far away to me, and the idea of entering the hard electrical field of the shop itself was daunting, quite apart from the culture shock. Nevertheless, I liked going for the long, leisurely drive, half an hour there and half an hour back through thirty miles of mallee and sandalwood wilderness, with its abundance of wild flowers in late winter and spring.

Unfortunately, the enchantment began to forbid these trips. When one was planned I'd be unable to rise, to get up out of bed, even to lift my head. I'd apologize to Helen for the last minute change of plans—she was getting used to it—and when she'd driven off and the sound of the old Jeep was fading away in a cloud of dust down the half-mile track to the dirt road, I'd miraculously find the torpor lifting until I could sit up again and dialogue with my mirror.

Sometimes I'd lift my head up from some activity and the caravan walls would dim, fading out of sight as a misty view of that other, aerial world took its place. This place was a flat landscape, and supported little vegetation except green-grey grass. Here, low rises and dips were the only features except for grey and blue lagoons and the same hazy smoky blue of the sky that I'd seen on that magical sprint some twenty-four years previously.

Other times I'd step outside and unexpectedly see not the campfire, fenced garden and limestone flats of home, but buildings, a street, figures coming and going and I'd hear the muted voices of other worlds.

I began to long for pause: not for freedom or evasion of these marvellous, if involuntary, experiences, but just the chance to take stock, to compare notes with other seers, and to take the occasional reality check.

I wanted to read books, do some research, but this was not permitted. "Focus on what you already know," the faerie told me. So I'd riffle through my sparse store of human trivia on faeries, and attempt to piece it all together into something that made sense. It wasn't anything to do with the supernatural, which somehow made it easier, at least in the case of faeries. I knew of only one kind of faerie, and that was the kind I was with: the "Tinkerbell" type. Everything I knew about them came from children's faerie fiction.

As I'd done with faerie art, I focused on the tradition of faerie fiction making, and saw in panorama all the people in the long and specialized tradition of writing about faerie. I felt a connection with each author's life. His or her growing up was often nourished imaginatively by the faeries as mine had been, and their writing had been inspired by the winged creatures, subconsciously informed by them, so that the authors produced their fictional faeries in such a manner that our conscious appreciation of them, as fiction, remains accordant with our subliminal knowledge of the reality. In just such an atmosphere, Shakespeare's Peaseblossom, Cobweb, Moth and Mustardseed, as well as J. M. Barrie's Tinkerbell and the whole genre of gauzy-winged, gossamer-gowned, feelered, and flower-oriented diminutive faeries, emerged. These well-known characters, dear to literature, and especially to children's literature, were birthed into human fantasy by the faeries themselves.

We humans tend to think of ourselves as great lumps of materiality, slow-witted, dull-sensed, unmagical, and powerless, at least compared with faeries and elementals and their ilk. In fact, we are every bit as magical as they are, if only we could wake up to it. In order to see the various beings who were presented to me during this time, I am being forced to find and integrate all my selves, the many functions of my mind, the many bodies of my being. It's an enormous task, and will take me more than this one life span to achieve: or perhaps its a task that is never really finished for anyone.

Studying myself as an example of a human being, I was beginning to see the fabric of human culture in a completely new way. In my primary consciousness I was becoming aware of conversations taking place on another level of consciousness between myself and corresponding levels of consciousness in other people. This occurred not only with Helen, who was nearby, but also with friends and acquaintances who lived thirty or ninety or a few thousand miles away, and not only with humans but also with animals, like my cats, my dog, and my goats. Taking myself and my contacts to be typical, this gave me a vastly expanded sense of what it is to be human.

A logical next step was to extend this new understanding from small groups to the greater community: to cities, cultures, groups of nations, and ultimately to the whole of human interaction. I saw the planet leap into a new and exciting focus, my view of its thin, fragmentary, conflict-ridden discourse of normal consciousness blossoming into the vital, diverse, multidimentionality of rich experience that was now obviously the sparkling, magical, coherent mind of one great, sentient being, Gaia. And of course, she was aware of me, as she is of all her beings. She came to my mind as a wise, yet playful intelligence, old, young and ageless all at once. She was beautiful, ugly and everything

in between, communicating through shapeshifting, projected images, thought and words. These communications
were humorous and loving, and suffused with the kind of
sustaining joy that restores faith in the future of our planet.

Chapter 7
The Faerie in the Jar

One day I woke with a panicky sense of urgency. I sat up and looked in the mirror, sensing someone or something making a huge effort, almost electrical with agitation and excitement. There was fear, a sense of danger, of threat: this other's, or mine. Ultimately it was my own share of it that threw me into a state of confusion, and that made me panic all the more. I knew that this was one of those days when the enchantment would not permit me to go outside. Unable to escape, I lay down and shut my eyes.

They wouldn't stay closed. Against my will they flitted anxiously about the caravan, from mirror to wall to plants to ceiling, until they came to rest on a flower pot in which I was trying to start leaf cuttings of begonias. To protect them from the dry heat of early summer, I'd covered them with an inverted, wide- necked jar. In the sunlight streaming in through my window at that hour of the morning it looked very beautiful, reflecting the many colours of my walls and ceiling the way clear glass does, and throwing a delicate, translucent shadow on the table-top behind it. I watched it for a while, and then began to notice a tiny movement within the jar, just a slight shifting of light across light, a tremor of subtle energy, the merest ripple in the air.

At first I thought it was some activity in the life field of the plantlets, and I settled back to watch it. But the movement increased, the colour and texture deepened, and then I underwent that change in perception that occurs when the Aerial beings connect with someone decisively enough to engage their subtle senses. There, briefly visible in the jar, was a highly excited faerie, desperately trying to tell me something. There seemed to be no way I could find out what it was.

Anxiety has its cutoff point. I decided that for the sake of my sanity, this had to be some kind of joke. Okay. I was willing to go along with a joke.

"Wow," I gloated, "a real faerie in a jar, eh? Think how much I could make out of this. Charge people so much a look. I'll be rich! All I have to do is find a way to make her visible to ordinary people. What fun!"

Despite my jest, my mirth wasn't wholehearted. I was frightened. For some reason I next chose to go into denial on the whole issue. There was no faerie in that jar. I was angry. I could easily believe in these beings and their dances and magic moonbeams, but not in this old faerie-trapped-in-a-jar cliché. I closed my aerial eyes and turned away from my mirror, ignoring my plants, especially the begonia leaf-cuttings. As usual when I wanted to block any possible telepathy I sang silently in my head until, as often happens when you sing silent songs, one song took over so that I found one snatch of it repeating itself over and over. It was a song by the songwriter Donovan, "The Tinker and the Crab." I'd forgotten almost all of it except for the very end, in which the title is enigmatically repeated three times. To clear my head I let the song speak to me. In this song, "Tinker," incidentally, means one of the Romany people.

I have almost certainly inherited a thread of Romany blood through my mother's father's mother. I therefore feel a strong sense of kinship with them, and often think about the specific nature of my inheritance from them. I share their sense of beauty, their pride, their power, their wisdom, and share also in the pain of their persecution. As I let my thoughts carry me along from one folkloric reference to another, trying to feel these connections, I raised my hands in an involuntary gesture and made a crab-like movement with my thumbs and forefingers—and felt myself tug at the fabric of reality.

Crabs tug like this at their environment, perhaps magically as well as physically, to attract their prey to them. Again I saw the faerie in the jar, and I was sure that she was real, trapped in that jar, and that I was to blame. To fill my subconscious need I had somehow used the inherited Romany magic to abduct this innocent faerie from among her helpless companions and spirit her into this jar so that I could interrogate her.

This was an unpalatable thought, so I rejected it. Then I gradually began again to acknowledge the fact of the faerie's captivity, and to address first glances, then apologies, and finally questions to her. After all, she was here, captive, and I didn't know how to release her without harming her, for it soon became obvious to me that behind the glass shield she had a degree of protection from the blasts, gales, and jets of energy that my human eyes emit in response to my emotions. I could look at her through the glass without distorting her too much, too; it helped to balance the natural tendency humans have to psycho-kinetically help things to look as they "should" look which is all right for material objects and beings, but tends to distort the finer substances of aerial beings. I began to feel justified. I rationalised that I was only doing to her what she and her companions had been doing to me for years, giving her a tiny dose of her own medicine.

Never had communication between faeries and me been better. I considered that she owed me at least a couple of long interviews. So I ,commenced: "Exactly what is your connection with flowers?" Her answers flowed like complex streams of subtly structured thought in my mind, silken and glossy. It was visual, like watching a film, but soundless, with panoramas of those organically fluid thoughtscapes that characterize faerie thought transference. I was held, willingly enough, in trance by her magical power, although what she was saying was fascinating in its own right. The gist of it was as follows:

"The plants are the physical expression of spiritualities. All material things are, even a piece of aluminium foil is the manifestation of its own spirituality. Hold it," she said. "Feel it. Put it against your lips, your forehead, feel it in your hand without seeing it. Let it affect your mood, your facial expression. Become sensitive, just for a moment, to its effect upon your mentality, the cast of your thoughts, the attitudes you adopt. Feel for its musical tone in you, and its melody. That's an example of a chemically simple substance. Imagine, now, that aluminium as part of a complex substance, pooling its spirituality, blending it with that of the greater world. Then you can begin to understand the spirituality of more complex things, living things, flowers, personalities."

The faeries' personalities, I learned, are generated in the moon's innermost core, the moon's equivalent of Tartarus, the earthly dwelling place of the Titans of Greek mythology. This might be why Shakespeare was inspired to call his faerie queen Titania. Their spirituality is then manifested first on the moon's Aerial plane as the primal faerie archetypes. They process various energies, feeding themselves to enable them to "go forth and multiply." Earth generated her first humans in a similar way. These first faeries are, unlike the first humans, all female, reproducing by an asexual process. As each becomes more and more complex, she divides herself in an orderly kind of schizophre-

83

nia, projecting an alter ego that also becomes "flesh" and achieves autonomy. This type is the type I was now interviewing. They are winged, about seven or eight inches high, and they inhabit the aerial plane, feeding on radiances and energies of various kinds.

These aerial beings feel themselves and their environment to be as substantial as we do ours. As the faerie in the jar showed me, we appear wraithlike and our forms vaporous and changeable to them. Their bodies, like ours, are cellular, their cells made of Aerial atoms, knotted up just as ours are into genes, chromosomes and the whole mechanistic chemistry of all truly biological beings, tailor-made to express the spirituality that is unique to the moon.

However, the moon is another planet, and its essential spirituality embraces many qualities that are quite alien to the earth, and even at odds with it. When a moon native enters the life-field of the Earth there is a powerful force acting upon her to pull her genetics, which are generating an alien spirituality, into harmony with the spirituality of the Earth, to negate her distinctively moon-born qualities and impose Earthly qualities upon her. Mass mutations, not necessarily in their interests, would affect faerie populations on Earth if they did not take measures to prevent them. Their faerieland on the Earth's Aerial plane is within a constantly maintained force field that protects it from the mutative force of the Earth's life-field, as well as keeping them from acting as an irritant to the Earth. Outside it, faeries also establish circles of protection around themselves and their activities that are temporary. Faerie rings, indeed.

"Yes," I say, "but what about the flowers?"

Oh yes, we're coming to that.

Chapter 8
Of Plants and Flowers

When human beings first walked on the moon, their genetic impact on the moon, and its effect on them, was very strong. Just as the moon itself and a great many faeries cooperated to dance the faerie moonbeam path to the Earth that night when I saw all those faeries coming into our planet, so millions of television viewers all over the world watched our first astronauts land on the terrestrial surface of the moon, lending our combined mental and psychic powers from all over the world to the project .

The astronauts were profoundly affected, not just emotionally, but physically, too, as they responded to the soul and spirit energies of the life field of the material sphere of the moon. The moon's subsequent reaction to a quick succession of human visitors was so complex and lengthy that we stopped after only a few years and have not resumed, even thirty years later. Stranger still, hardly anybody takes more than a passing interest in the reason why something so vital to science and symbolically powerful to humanity should have petered out so ignominiously. Subconsciously we know the reason: the energetic discord between our two planets is deeply jarring, and we need time to recover from it as much as the moon does.

So, from within her protected faerieland on the aerial plane, if a moon-born faerie wishes to become adapted to conditions on Earth—and that's what she's here to do— she must either accept a succession of mutations to become like an Earth being, losing her feelers, wings, and many of her faculties, including access to her race memories and the collective spirit of faeries of the moon, or persuade the Earth to mutate to accommodate faerie spirituality as it is, incorporating into her own biome the genes that will express distinctively moon-faerie qualities.

This latter option is the one that interests me here, although both options are taken up, along with a whole array of compromises in between. A complete mutation takes an enormous amount of work, energy, and time, and no faerie could stay put long enough to achieve it. Nor could she endure the stress. Instead, each faerie displays one significant quality which she must have to express her faerie nature on Earth. The new information diffuses through the myriad channels of communication throughout the world, and the work begins, through her, for all faeries.

Every sphere responds in its own way. On the terrestrial sphere, the focus is on flowers. First, a flower that naturally manifests a quality most like the faerie quality in question is found. Then it is subjected, from the communal level down to the level of individuals, to calculated stresses and vexations which will produce in it the desired mutation: that which causes its genome to incorporate the faerie quality itself.

Now, as seriously out of harmony with the Earth's native spirituality as the faerie quality might be, it must be held in the earth's collective consciousness perhaps for centuries, while the Earth adapts to it. Various strategies besides faerie dances are employed. For example, people might blow the seeds from a dandelion stalk while fixing their mind on the idea of clock time, because the mode of time structuring is being moulded into the dandelion's genome in such a way as to give future faeries our sense of linear time, of history, and of time-event relationships, which they otherwise lack.

Once such a mutation is completed, the faeries, still in their protected environment, are now able to dance themselves into a spiritual accord with the plant, and when that accord is perfect, they can merge their own being with that of the plant. Their presence in their aerial faerieland wanes, and in the terrestrial flower a heightened intensity reveals to the sensitive seer the presence of the faerie, translocated as easily as if she'd stepped through a doorway. At this stage, she can access only limited sensations from the plant's own sensory systems. If she wants more than this from the plant, she must modify it from within, or by dancing.

Meanwhile, within the Earth-born flower, the moon-born faerie is able to bring her own spiritual nature more into harmony with the Earth's.

This takes compromise: the Earth, having gone so far out of her way to accommodate the faerie, requires that the faerie extend herself to meet it. Consequently, it takes a succession of such faerie visits to a large number of flowers of that species, over a long period of time, to induce the requisite mutation and hold it in place. That is, the change must be sufficient to bring about a mutation at the communal, species level: when it reaches this point, the effect becomes diffused throughout the Earth. No longer localized in a single plant species, effects are felt in everything from dog-clipping fashions to racehorse names, introducing a new lilt into pop-songs, a new rhythm to lawnmower engines, a minute alteration to the pattern on a moth's wings. For the sake of simplicity I have described a single mutation, although of course each faerie must undergo a number of mutations. Her genome contains not one or two but many moon-specific genes which are still stressful and vexing to the beings of planet Earth.

"Why flowers?" I asked her. "Why not moths, say, or fish, or birds?"

Plants, I learned, are more tolerant of mutations that may not necessarily be in their own interests. Their beauty and accessibility means that humans will enjoy cooperating with faeries in working with them. And plants themselves can benefit in many ways. The integration of our two planets, Earth and the moon, is a healing phenomenon, and plants are the first to benefit. They are also able to absorb large amounts of mutagenic force, proliferating variant after variant and doing it relatively stresslessly. The result is beauty, not disease, as it would be in less flexible animal species.

A glance at a flower catalogue will tell you how far we've come with these mutants and variants. They're not all for the sake of faeries, but many of them are. So there are now many faeries who have a certain amount of freedom on Earth. Their flowers will let them step out into their terrestrial environment, and in congenial gardens all over the world. They are in the centuries-long process of acclimatising themselves to terrestrial conditions. Simultaneously, they are accustoming the terrestrial ecosystems to their presence and their energies. Faeries do a lot of work with the energies and radiance they bring into the Earth from other planets, other stars, and other cosmic sources. They easily spin themselves from one energy level to another, bringing in strands of aether, wisps of aerial substance. These they intensify or moderate, weaving into the terrestrial environment the energies of distant planets, other dimensions, and universes beyond our ken, as we ourselves do, mostly without realizing it. Some of this a seer can see or sense in the slightly altered atmosphere in a garden, especially at night under a full or otherwise favourable moon.

There's a lot more than energy being transferred. Plants

serve many more than their own ends. That is, every atom in existence carries a memory trace of every situation it's ever been in, beginning with the Big Bang, to its vastly convoluted journey through time and space, through its evolution in all kinds of cosmic situations, until it has reached its present situation.

These memory traces, for example, unique to each atom, combine with the memory traces, of every other atom in a plant, to make up the resources of the plant's "id". The plant itself has its own unique race memories as well, which are resources for the plant's own soul. Consequently, while an atom is absorbing the huge amount of data in the race memory of, say, a larkspur, which may include the whole evolution of plant-life on Earth and more, the larkspur is constantly availing itself of the accumulated memory traces that each of its atoms bears. How much of this process is conscious varies from one species to another. In plants this process is not regulated, except in rather general ways, while in faeries it is subject to the same kinds of filtration, organization and selection as it is in human beings. So, much to the benefit of plants, the faeries are deliberately perusing, purifying, judiciously adding and modifying, and generally manipulating the atom memory of every plant they enter. In time, they will have helped plants to express their own individual and collective wisdoms through their own vegetal bodies as we humans do through our animal bodies, instead of from their souls only.

To a faerie, every plant is like a vast garden of atoms and

molecules. All these need pruning, tending, weeding, their quarrels settled, their hurt parts sought out and soothed. This is the same whether it is a normally robust sulphur being, spiritually taunted by its aluminium neighbour's spiky little rays, or the endemic pain of an entire element, such as boron, all of whose atoms hurt. "Did you know that sulphur is hairy?" a faerie once asked me. Another time, she noted, giggling "Proteins wriggle. "

Faeries often project images of flowers to me, and I dare say to other gardeners, too, asking me to add my energy to their own, to play the radiance of my spontaneous reaction to its shape, colour, and general appearance over it, to bless it and give it a dose of a medicinal input from me.

Faeries do work intensively with plants, then, at least those that serve their own needs, but so do we humans. We're conscious of only a fragment of the work we do with plants. Despite our obsession with gardening, human beings are not plant spirits, and neither are the faeries of the moon. While any gardener might stop and pass the time of day with anyone who might be interested, and will freely share his or her knowledge of plants, only a few are specialized as guides in the world of plants. The same is true of faeries. We need only to overcome basic energetic incompatibilities and establish a good working relationship on the conscious level, extending the one we can now have on the aerial level, to become comfortably aware of faeries in our daily lives.

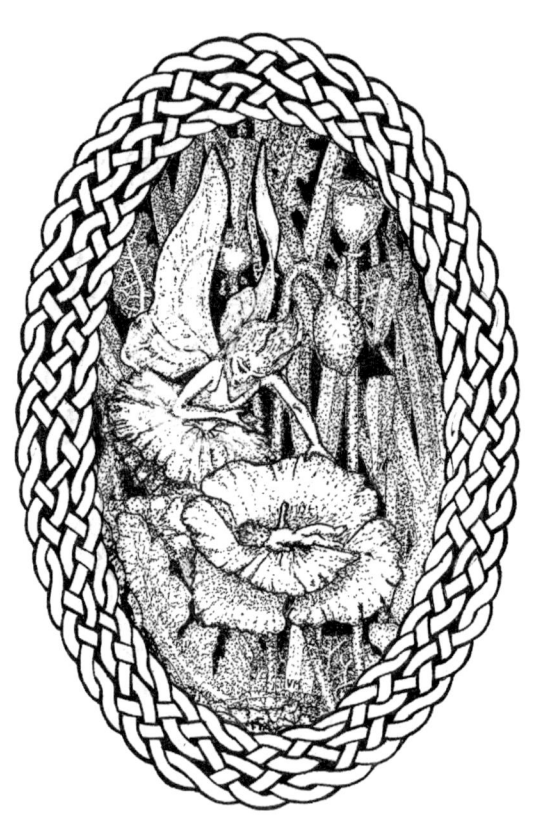

Chapter 9
Born From Flowers

One afternoon in early spring the weather was clear and sparkling, and it was impossible not to feel good with the ground still soft underfoot from the last of the winter rains, the mosses on the shady side of the wattle bushes still bright and velvety. The grass was fresh and green, the bees and hoverflies were at the waterbush flowers, and the tiny, starry, blue, white, and yellow wild flowers were every-where among the silvery plumes of speargrass. I was walking across the limestone towards the mallee in search of certain herbs, and keeping an eye out for mushrooms.

Looking up, I saw a hole opening up in the air in front of me. It appeared to be the mouth of a long curving tunnel. After all these years of experiencing things like that, I'm not afraid any more, so I stopped and waited. At the end of the tunnel a large flower like a hibiscus formed. It travelled rapidly along the tunnel towards me, changing as it came, until by the time it reached the mouth of the tunnel it was a completely different flower, rather like a very large pansy. Its diameter was about my height. All changes in colour, shape, size and texture had happened perfectly smoothly and fluidly, through a series of tiny, graduated alterations from one actual flower form to another, each one a specimen of an existing flower species. The process must have included a hundred or more.

The flower seemed to have come from an enormous distance, perhaps across several thousand miles, and from another time, another plane of existence. I can scarcely say how I sensed all this. It seemed to be demonstrating for me something the faeries had told me about but had not been able to show me. Certainly what it was doing was beautiful, mesmerisingly so. The faerie himself, for that's what it was, of course, soon stepped out of the final flower and laughing, gave me an old-fashioned deep bow, with a series of ornamental flourishes that made him look like an extravagantly ruffled, pink sweet pea. Then he disappeared.

This demonstration unfolded in my mind over the next few days, and it did indeed have to do with their teachings. That flow of flowers becomes possible for faeries when all the flowers are attunable and when they are all arranged in the right relationships to one another in the mind of the adept. For example, a faerie attuned to the dandelion flower, whose genetics encode the requisite dandelion qualities, may enter a dandelion through the communal idea of flowers or through an individual flower, or even through a photograph, a suitable sketch, or an artificial representation of a dandelion flower. She could move by a slight, exquisitely calculated shift of emphasis into a sow thistle and thus flow through into marigold, then into sunflowers, and work her way smoothly through to the cone-flower. At any point she has a multitude of choices.

From cone-flower, for example, she might flow into Australian wild flowers via the big banksia, through grevillias, melaleuca, callistemons and the petal-less eucalypts and acacias—or else veer off into pinecones, stonecrops, succulents or cactuses, or even into fungi and mosses. Of course, there are an infinite number of sequences.

Eventually she could reach any individual flower in the biome reasonably rapidly from any other flower anywhere on Earth, scrolling through till she found the location she wanted. Since distance is no object, what about other planets? Theoretically, she could locate, scroll her way through to, and emerge from, any flower on any plant anywhere in the universe as easily as you can now make a phone call, except it's not just her voice she would transmit, it's herself.

Let's get back, now, to flower faerie being and to the faerie in the jar, whose discourse triggered this memory. Faeries have a way of establishing an enchantment, with your full consent and awareness, and then without warning deepening it into a kind of second reality in which you become as completely absorbed, and as completely convinced, as you are by dreams. It makes one easily sidetracked, and my faeries were taking full advantage of that.

Without having any clear memory of a transition, I went from being the observer of faerie thoughtscapes to being an active inhabitant of a portion of that thoughtscape, which had incidentally become a whole other reality. Still kneeling on my bed that morning, I held an easy and quite natural-feeling conversation with a large number of new, alien beings whom I scarcely recognised as faeries. They were close to me, and yet they were simultaneously in parks and gardens throughout the world. They were no size, or any size, nowhere, yet everywhere. It was like a cyberspace meeting, except it was psycho-space, and they were intermittently visible.

I experienced myself as a nice, ordinary human woman walking in a public garden. I would bend to admire a flower and I would see, yet not be aware of seeing, one of these strange little beings drawing me towards it with its large alien eyes. There'd be a chill like fear in my stomach. Yes, fear. Then the being would flash at me an image of a flower, an image full of potency over and above that which real flowers have, and instead of staying where it formed, it would fly toward me.

Before I could do anything to stop it, it would engulf me and become one with my own energy field. The impact of these flowers was powerful, like a dose of strong medicine, and I wasn't altogether sure that it was good medicine every time. A geranium gave me good vision, but a sense of limitation and frustration as well. Sweet peas made me feel frivolous and unsound in some way. A carnation made me cautious and suspicious.

The worst of it was feeling as if I was at the mercy of these strange little beings, having my energy field manipulated by them without any assurance that they knew what they were doing. I finally protested. They countered that these flowers were blessings, to make me mutate so that I could be more in tune with flowers. They were gifts, psychic resources of great value. They did use words, but I remember not words but an over-current of unverbalized meaning.

I replied, regretting my school-marmish tone, that my freedom of choice was vital to my welfare. We argued back and forth for a while, and eventually began to understand each other a little better, and to come to terms. They agreed, finally, to simply show the flower to a human being as an image suspended in midair, and invite the person to accept it or not as they chose. I had a feeling that people do understand these flower energies and have a sense of what they do or don't want of them. I even remember having a particular wish for a white arum lily, which was duly given, though I later progressed to a bearded iris: and I felt healthy changes to my aura with each influx of specific flower power.

All the while, these strange, compelling little beings responded to me like children, demonstrating an earnest wish to please me. They made their flower images, offered them, and were very proud and pleased when I approved. My acceptance of the iris had assured them that they would not simply be ignored and rejected. It was a fact that I'd needed it.

Nevertheless, I still wasn't sure what they were. If faeries, what kind of faeries? These faeries were not the shrewd, sophisticated, dry-witted faeries to which I was accustomed. They were much smaller, with faces somewhere between the extreme alienness of the moon faeries and the cute appeal of human infants, with small wings, feelers and ear-tips, and faerie eyes and mouths in otherwise human faces.

"What," I asked the faerie in the jar, "are they?" I suppose I'd been with them for about an hour.

"Our babies," she explained.

"They're boys as well as girls. Born," she said, "from flowers."

I asked her to explain. She proceeded again to let her flow of thought into my mind. I sat crouched upon my bed with my knees drawn up under me, my chin in my hands, and I absorbed what she showed me, mesmerised as I was by the spell she cast. I could watch her thoughts as easily as you view a film.

"The flow of flowers," she began, "demands an ability to form an intense relationship with the flower, a relationship of pure love and total surrender like that which frightened you when you came close to the violet that day. It also requires the cooperation of anyone else who might have a legitimate interest in the plant's evolution. While faeries are deeply absorbed in the plant, the plant is equally absorbed in the faeries. It has their imprint." I knew this, recalling my experience with the violet. I came to learn that, even when there is no faerie within a much-frequented plant, the plant will still be so fraught with faerie spirituality that it will seem to be inhabited. It is an easy matter, then, for a group of faeries to bring their powers to bear on such a plant to induce it to supply a phantomlike form, or several identical phantomlike forms, to capture this formless faerie spirit. This or these phantoms are nourished, nursed and nurtured into life, and they begin to function as beings in their own right, while still within the plant. This incubation occurs while the plant is not in flower. At this stage it is still unstable and, since it is destined to inhabit the terrestrial planet as an Aerial being, it needs the strong earthly qualities of Earthborn human beings, so the souls of human children are passed through the flower to impose their forms upon the foetal faeries.

These children are of course carefully selected. They must be willing. They must be able to cooperate with faeries on subliminal levels through play, fantasy and dreams. Their parents must be willing to permit the faeries access to their child, because, as magical as faeries might be, for psychic violence and aggression nothing beats a human mother in defence of her young, unaware of it though she might be. This happens, furthermore, in the realms of the soul: while a small child's material body may be new, and her mind may be functioning through the cerebral neurology specific to childhood, with its characteristic vulnerabilities and trust, her soul is as old, perhaps, as humanity itself, having evolved through many lifetimes, accumulating wisdom and knowledge as it grows. Normally, a soul will have some history of co-evolution with faeries, and some souls are born again and again into cultures that interface intensely with faeries, whether on conscious or subconscious levels. In our culture, it is normal to put children into contact with the faerie realm through story books and guided play. Every child knows that faeries slide down moonbeams, dance at midnight, and grant wishes with a wave of their magic wands. Tinkerbell is loved by all. In shamanistic cultures, people might achieve conscious accord with a faeried flower in ritual dance, perhaps while in trance, but in our culture, the child concerned is more likely to achieve it in creative dance and play supervised by a kindergarten teacher. The child might be instructed to "be" a little flower bud on its stem, to expand himself slowly like an opening flower, to rise up and spread out his arms and fingers like the big, beautiful, petals of a flower. It's important to the faerie that these helping children should be in a joyous, loving mood, since their soul-imprint will become a feature of the new hybrid faerie's being, and it must be pure and acting out of love.

Of course, this is the ideal, and faeries are idealists to say the least but our planet is far from ideal. We do operate via this conscious-subconscious split, and are often driven by our own subconscious purposes far more powerfully than, and sometimes in conflict with, our conscious ones. It is from clashes of this sort that most of our quarrels with faeries arise, but, bitter as they sometimes get, they seldom run deep.

As these hybridizations happen over thousands of years, they constitute a veritable marriage of the Earth and the Moon, although in some ways it's more like the fusion of gametes to form a zygote during the fertilization of an egg. Most of the process takes place throughout the species, the action moving from one favourably situated plant to another over a period of several months or even years. The actual birth, however, occurs in a selected flower bud.

It takes the time from the formation of the bud to the peak of its blossoming for the new faerie to be concentrated there and to emerge.

Some flowers, dandelions for example, produce only boys; daffodils produce boys and girls; hyacinths produce girls. Tansy, feverfew and thyme are examples of plants that faeries do not frequent, although they benefit from their presence in gardens.

Plants that are native to Australia produce faeries with an Aboriginal cast to their features; Japanese plants Asian features; African African; and so on. The spiritual nature of the plant also determines the apparent age of the new faerie. From an eucalypt blossom she or he will emerge as a very young child; from a hyacinth, as an older child of about five to ten years, depending on the individual hyacinth. The faerie children range in height from two to three inches to about six. At first they strongly exhibit the qualities of their parent plant, and they stay close to it, taking refuge within it whenever they feel the need, and travelling from place to place through its flowers. Later they develop their affinities with other plants and become more free.

"Does this mean they're stuck in their plants when they're not in flower?" I asked.

"Yes, it does, as if dormant. That's why it matters so much to have their flowers in both hemispheres, and to extend their flowering periods as much as possible. In the future, thousands of species of flowers will bloom year round on every continent, and they'll be far more beautiful than they are now." Like newborn humans, then, faerie infants spend most of their time asleep and dreaming.

I saw her head jerk as if she were referring to an extant future somewhere over her left shoulder and sensed in her manner a familiarity with it, as if it were a place she'd often visited. Perhaps I even glimpsed it, stretching away like a landscape behind her.

"Is that a prophecy?" I asked her.

She nodded:"yes".

Chapter 10
Flower Power

One day, while I was out walking, a few years after this interview, my eyes flitted over the ground to gauge what new plants may have taken advantage of our short desert winter, with its mild, rainy days and warm sunny interludes, to spread their leaves and bloom their blooms. I noticed a lot of aerial movement centred around a little native plant of the family violaceae, with its small rosette of leaves flat to the ground and its hair-thin stem curving elegantly up to a tiny, sunny yellow flower with irregular lower petals rolled up and grooved like a little clenched fist.

There were three or four faeries around it which I dimly saw, but as I looked carefully, straining everything not to buffet them with a blast of my glance, one of them flashed plainly into view for a split second, just long enough for her to register clearly in my sight. She was a broadly smiling faerie with Aborigine features, her skin a warm dark brown, her hair a mass of dark curls. If she had feelers I didn't see them. She was much more human than those

I'd encountered in the park, representing a further stage in their humanward evolution. She came across as a ten or eleven year old, though I had the impression that her companions were different ages, and different colours, too.

She was wearing a kind of grey tunic and no shoes. She had her right fist up, raised in the power sign of the liberation movements and civil rights movements. Her voice buzzed in the air: "Fey Liberation!" She flourished her fist, in unmistakable feisty imitation of her flower. I was delighted. There were many of these flowers growing in that area and I picked one, examined it, and ate it. It had a mild, pleasant flavour.

The faeries had vanished, so I continued my walk.

Under the influence of that flower's spiritual power, I found myself drawn over the next few days to review my mind set concerning my psychic experiences from a new "Fey Liberationist" position, which spelled itself out in my mind eloquently as I did so.

It was timely. I began to see what strenuous efforts I underwent to scrutinize, analyse, and dissect every vision, every instance of telepathy, clairaudience, and clairvoyance I experienced. I had subjected it all to the kind of scrupulous examination to which I imagined someone with a rigorous training in orthodox psychiatry would subject it. I tried to imagine what popular psychology would do with it, or what people in general, rationalists, sceptics, or other more credulous people, would make of an account of the psychic experiences I normally have each day.

Since Findhorn, some might give credence to the flower faeries, but most would reject the idea that they or their ancestors had originated on the moon. Some might believe that I'd seen faeries, but not that I communicate regularly with them with more ease and comfort that I normally enjoy with other people, nor might they believe the things I've been taught by faeries.

In short, I realized I had always tried to look at my own inner experience through everyone's hypothetical eyes except my own, trying to veto, censor, and tailor my experience to satisfy everyone else's sense of the credible, while scarcely giving my own opinions about it houseroom.

If any of the very few people I still had anything to do with, including my own family, asked me what I was doing and why I wasn't working, I would simply tell them what I imagined their diagnosis would be: that I was schizophrenic, or that I had a neurological disorder that was causing hallucinations. If schizophrenic means psychic, or having psychic perceptions that are as real as normal perceptions, maybe I am schizophrenic. Why, though, might I be categorized along with seriously dysfunctional mentalities, the criminally insane, brain-damaged, and emotionally distraught people? Perceiving other worlds that actually do exist can hardly be called a neurological disorder. I have remained rational throughout, my critical faculties working, my mind alert and fully functional, thinking clearly and rationally about the extraordinary experiences I have had. I was always able to distinguish between socially acceptable topics of conversation and unacceptable ones whenever I had to, and was always able to pass myself off as "normal" whenever anyone dropped in for a social or business visit. Whatever I was, I was not insane.

What, I asked myself, of the shamanisms of the world, the large number of cultures past and present, including the ancient Hebrews, Elijah and Ezekiel and their tradition, and even the Catholic Church with its sainted visionaries? Too, there are witches, witch doctors, and shamans whose extraordinary visions are still valued in many extant cultures all over the world today.

How dare, I thought, a handful of materialistic cynics tyrannise our cultures' seers for so long in the name of reason! It was, I decided, utterly unreasonable of them! And so in my mind the healing polemic unfurled itself like a graceful flower, upright on its elegantly curved stem, liberating, empowering, refreshing and real, and all in response to some faerie-wrought molecules in the cytoplasm of that little fey power flower.

There are times when I love the faeries with all my heart and soul.

I have digressed from the faerie in the jar again, and it is time we got back to her, back to the caravan and the morning light.

Under her spell, I began to muse upon the increasing frequency of moon-faeries, their flower-born children, and various other hybrids they had shown me. I saw their bodies achieving greater and greater density and visibility, until they became real flesh and blood as solid as I am.

She made me understand that faerie lands and faerie havens are already being established in the material world, some in remote parts of wildernesses and some in city parks, private gardens and on apartment balconies in the hearts of our biggest cities.

These gardens and wild places are already harbouring fairly large populations of faeries, whom we can only perceive through our psychic senses. Eventually they will come to be plainly visible, touchable, biological, material beings, although able to shift back through the spectrum to their own aerial forms, and again back to the material at will.

Some of these faeries will want to use their material havens as a kind of thoroughfare to the worlds below— the inner worlds of the Earthly spheres. They will deep-dive from our level to the Hadean world, where the Tuatha de Danaan, the ancient Romans' heroes, and the champions of other ancient warrior races went when they died.

They will travel deeper, into Tartarus, a land so deep below this one that, according to the ancient Greeks, it would take an anvil nine days falling to arrive there. It's a land of giant Titans, archetypal people who keep the knowledge of this planet's deepest mysteries.

These places are real. People do get reborn or re-manifested in these worlds after they've died.

Some faeries will want to remain free to climb up and down this "Jacob's ladder" from the lowest end of the spectrum to the highest, but others will choose to focus exclusively on just on level, and some of these will choose the material plane, becoming fully material beings in the course of a few thousand years. Incarnating over several lifetimes as tiny human-like beings, these faeries will come under the genetic pull and command of the material plane, and lose wings, antennae, and access to the higher wisdoms and faculties of the spirit, becoming in effect fallen faerie angels. In this way they will learn by immersion, for all faerie kind, all they'll need to know about the material reality to enable them to establish their own colonies of material, flesh and blood faeries on the material surface of the moon, their own planet of origin.

With the knowledge they gain as material beings, experiencing our physics, chemistry, biology, psychology, sociology and so on, they will go home and terraform the moon, taking with them a Noah's Ark of modified and miniaturized earth animals and plants with which, along with other life-forms from other sources, they will eventually create self-sustaining ecosystems over the entire material surface of the moon.

This is of course thousands or tens of thousands of years from now. They'll be assisted, as we are now, by their angel faeries and elementals. They will alter the moon's atmosphere, making it enough like Earth's to permit oceans and rivers to form, teletransporting the necessary liquids and gases, and even solids, from the stars, ice drifts in space, and clouds of cosmic dust. In other words, they will build their soils, their forests, their oceans and their clouds, out of stardust. She showed me these things in a series of sweeping images. They've already begun. There's the merest haze of an atmosphere there already.

Meanwhile, those faeries who are currently preparing to materialize on planet Earth will need our help to get here. That's why in many cultures, including Malaysian tradition, people traditionally build tiny houses or shrines for the faeries. I've seen faeries use the classic upturned terracotta flower pot with a big chip out of one side for the purpose, while the gardener, subliminally aware of the use the faeries are putting it to, is careful not to disturb it. In my garden they used the space under the large fronds of a big, airy fern, and this faerie I was communicating with had actually achieved visibility in my upturned jar.

Once they have the structure in place, they can project themselves into them and then endow them with force fields that will sustain them at energy levels more and more closely approximating our own, increasing their densities and shifting their vibrational rates down to the part of the spectrum of being that our senses are designed to perceive.

There flashed into my view a tiny bamboo house on a pole, with two faeries in it. One sat in the doorway, swinging her legs over the edge, while the other moved about rather gingerly inside.

Both looked a little grim, frowning at things, and gripping the doorpost and window frames as if they were afraid they might fly off the material plane and disappear. They appeared to be concentrating on getting a "grip" on our gravity, by tuning themselves to it in some way. "This will come soon," she said.

At the same time, people are crafting exquisite doll houses for them. When I was a child, they had used my doll's house as such a shrine, delighting in the funny blocky furniture and painted facades that were no use to them, and entwining their reality with my faerie-fantasies indulgently and affectionately. Nowadays, doll house hobbyists are more inclined to make their houses more "real," the furniture more in proportion, the materials more appropriate, real running water in the taps, hot and cold, and electric lights throughout.

Once enough faeries have been acclimatized in these houses they will begin to build their own, some by using materials available as we do, others by magically manifesting the materials and objects they need.

The faerie in the jar kept reminding me that we humans are also constantly magically working in the material world, modifying it, just by casting our gaze over things, by adopting different attitudes to things, and in myriad ways more subtle and yet more truly powerful than we can imagine. We too are reaching a level of evolution at which we will be able to exhibit the miraculous powers that have only ever been shown thus far on Earth through rare, exceptional individuals. This aspect of our evolution is being considerably speeded up by the near approach of the aerial beings, and others, to our sphere.

The work is not being done entirely by faeries and people. Gaia is aware of the faeries, and is preparing many tiny plants and miniaturizing many animals, including dogs, cats, horses, and pigs, for them. Faeries take great delight in these creatures and plants. I was shown a tiny white dog, very alert, mirthful and intelligent, and not more than an inch high.

As well, we're being psychologically prepared for these changes in myth and in literature. Thumbelina, Tom Thumb, and others like them turn every generation's childhood mind to the problems of the lifestyles awaiting extreme diminutives in the material world. Books like Mary Norton's "The Borrowers" series takes the logistics very seriously: in "The Borrowers Afield" we are presented with a minutely detailed investigation of the problem, following the lives of tiny humans who hunt for mice and sparrows for food and clothing, gather seeds and berries, and live in old boots and abandoned rabbit holes, desperately afraid of being seen. With skill the author brings the reader right into their world, while we watch them deal with predators such as cats, ferrets, eagles, hawks, grass snakes, and humans, in addition to the difficulties they have with the weather; freezing, flooding, and being buried in snow.

Real faeries will have to deal with these things, too, though they'll have more help than the Borrowers did. Our fictional diminutives, heroic and homely, help to provide archetypal images from which faeries can benefit in much the same way as we benefit from those we make for ourselves.

It took me a long time to absorb these facts, and my faerie lecturer had to repeat parts of it several times before I could grasp it all. I had a lot of resistance to overcome: it was too close to how I had attempted to depict them as a child, too much like the fantasies of my early childhood. Had I perhaps got my wires crossed and begun to draw material from my own imagination, preserved all these years and still active, for some reason, in the back of my mind? Was I creating delusions to enchant myself, instead of letting myself hear the real faerie I was with? I kept scrutinizing it in review, trying to see where her story left off and mine began, but it appeared to me to be seamless. I had, once or twice, a powerful urge to slam the door of disbelief on her then and there, but she would not disappear, and whenever I turned away from her she pulled my mind back to her with more magnetic power than I was able to resist. Either she had said all that, or she herself was not real, was merely the hallucination of a deranged mind, and I might as well go and live in a hospital for the insane, which is where most faerie seers end up.

Yet I knew she wasn't a delusion. It was not possible to doubt her reality, or the power she was exercising over me. As she was real, then, this revelation she was feeding me was true. To me now, it seems inevitable, it's the obvious direction for the co-evolution of our race to take, and by focusing our children's imagination on it, we are utilising one of the most powerful creative tools we've got.

Diminutive people, plants, animals. She let me think it over for a while, and I eventually asked her, "Will they have smaller atoms that we have, or would they have fewer atoms of the same size?"

"Fewer atoms," she said.

But that would mean less complex brains. She showed me how a simple brain could allow faeries unimpeded access to their own memories, and to the collective faerie consciousness and wisdom. There being no need to filter their perceptions and impressions through the complicated physiology of the human brain, they could be more direct, with greater awareness and direct access to wisdom, leaving them free to evolve in other directions of which I could not easily conceive.

I fell into a kind of trance again, perusing a three dimensional image of a human brain, comparing it with a faerie brain, and I recalled the instances I'd seen of remarkable intelligence in an eagle I once knew, in young Australian magpies I'd reared from rescued chicks, in a corella my brother once rescued. Even more to the point, I remembered the amazing intelligence and completeness of personality exhibited by three orphaned kangaroo joeys I'd reared, each one as rugged an individual as you'd ever wish to meet. Kangaroos are dismissed by scientists as "not intelligent" because they have small, apparently simple brains, yet they exhibit a lively intelligence when kept as pets, adapting easily to the unnatural conditions they encounter in a house and backyard environment, and learning with ease and great pleasure. I ended up staring intently at the faerie brain image, which I was now seeing with startling clarity and precision. In fact, this new dimension in my vision fascinated me almost as much as the floating three-dimensional image of the brain.

But the image of this brain began to worry me. It was too real to be so exposed, too vulnerable. I willed there to be a skull over it, and a scalpful of faerie hair, two ears upswept and pointed, two thin, insectile feelers. Then I let the large-eyed, bony, wrinkled little wedge of a face turn toward me to look at me. I let her show me her skinny little arms, her pale green dress, her skinny shoulders. It was the captive faerie, out of her jar without any difficulty.

That's when I understood that I'd been the captive all along. She'd set up her own "captivity," exploiting my inherited talent for her own use, and she'd let me bear that huge burden of guilt and confusion, using it to paralyse my will and bring me into her spell: a whole day spent in various depths of trance under the control of my captive captor. Now she, who earlier could not bear the least glance from my eyes, was sauntering about on the floor under my intent gaze as if it were the most comfortable place in the world to be.

Gesturing to crumbs on my table, she said, "So we will need these. " I understood: all the tiny berries, seeds, dewdrops, honey, pollen and nectar, and all the wide and varied delicate diet that human whimsy and children's fiction has proposed for them, will have a real function as these faeries work toward their adaptations to our Earth. By then, we too will have changed, will have learned to move our beings off the terrestrial plane and back at will, to explore other dimensions of this planet of ours, the worlds within worlds of Earth.

There I was again, staring through the faerie's mind into a future scape whose features I could barely begin to recognize. There was a moment of tension, and then she released me and was gone.

Chapter 11
The Lifting of the Spell

It was some months before the dreamy density of that enchantment wore off. To greet me in my recovered state were the cats, the dog, the goats, the garden again, and the long-suffering, patient Helen. For all their combined care, I went very nearly mad. I had suspended disbelief and deferred my emotional responses, and now the delayed reaction was huge. It was painful trying to bring the focus of my still-fascinated mind back to earthly things that had become alien to me, to force myself to descend back through the layers of consciousness that lie between aerial awareness and normal terrestrial awareness.

On the psychic levels that intervene, I was bombarded with a bewildering array of fake faeries by people I couldn't identify who wanted to believe I was a credulous fool who had never seen real faeries. I was threatened, tormented, and attempts made to force me to say there were no faeries of the moon, that I was merely one more mad woman, and belonged in a hospital for the insane. A prolonged effort, lasting for years, has been made, mostly on the astral plane, by some self-appointed arbiters of "normal society" to drive me mad, in order to discredit my stories about moon faeries and the Earth itself. This period was prolonged and complex and worth a whole book on its own. These conflicts are on-going, and take the form of voices in my head, with apparitions of hostile astral beings. But they are not unreasoning and progress towards peace and understanding is already happening. This faerie 'revival' is not a revival of mutant moronic babies, Ophelia-style madness and 'the falling sickness' and 'swimmings in the head' of past eras, and as fear is allayed, so hostility gives way to wonder and ultimately, to admissions of love.

In about 1990, when the worst was over, the faerie from my conversations returned to my caravan with a few companions, filling the space with their silken silveriness and bringing me to the brink of that swoony light-headedness that's like a sweet nausea. I was afraid but unable to resist their approach. The violent display of human fear of faeries that I had been witness to, and affected by, had changed me. In this deadly war, which is what it amounts to, I scarcely knew where my sympathies lay. I found myself snarling like a cornered faerie.

There passed through my mind image after image of human cruelty to faerie, enough to match theirs to us and more: faeries impaled on thorns, cursed into deformity, embedded in solid objects, kept immobile under spells, tormented in every conceivable way by the repressed, unrecognized, unconfessed magic of the men and women and children of ordinary, everyday, modern terrestrial Earth.

There were tense moments of silence that quivered with emotion following this flow of images. Hearing and seeing these faeries had become very difficult for me; my mind kept wandering. My fear was hard to control. Yet, at the climax of that strained silence, I at last heard the insectile vibration of her voice buzz past my ear. Addressing me as if I were the representative of all terrestrial people, she said, "True faeries *will* love you". And they vanished.

Epilogue

I didn't see another faerie until about nine years later, just before I began to write this book. Everything had changed. The eighties had altered me violently and profoundly. During the nineties I'd been slowly and strenuously working towards a new, more harmonious relationship with the human beings of terrestrial Earth. The person I now am has better health, is more self-empowered, and feels much less alienated.

I've always believed in love, but now I have a different idea of love, one that cloys less, that isn't calculated or competitive, that is less intrusive and much less demanding. When the faeries approach me I still wait for fear to rise from my subconscious, but now there isn't much there: there's mainly this feeling of love.

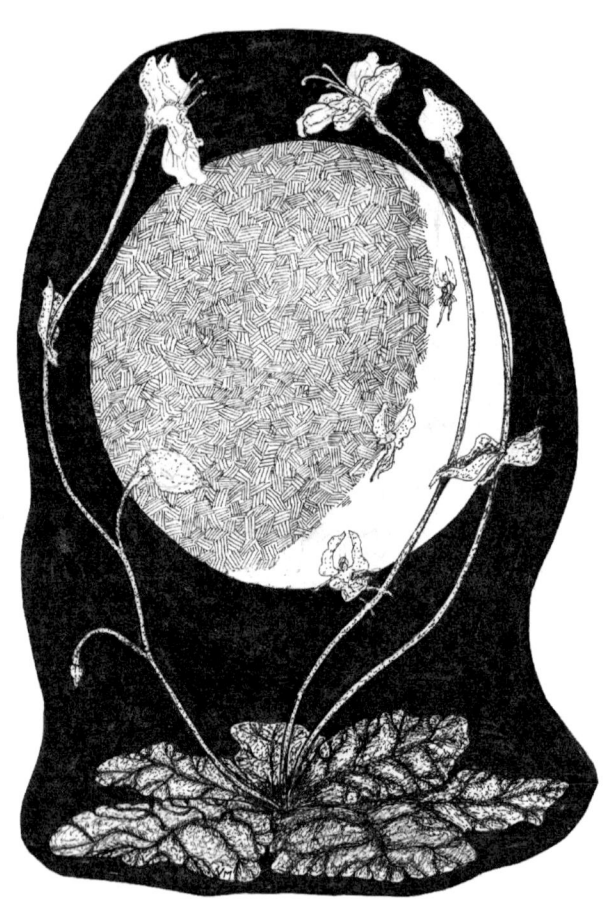

Appendix

The Spheres of the Earth and the Moon.

The substances of which the Universe is made are like the colours of a rainbow: a spectrum of many equally valid but different energy/substances, each one comprising a fully evolving universe in itself. I call these different universes 'realms'. Like the colours of rainbows which are seen when white light is split into its constituent radiances, these different energy/substances are all derived from one, their characteristics varying according to the vibrational rate of this 'arch-energy/substance'. If this stays below a certain critical point, it is formless and void, like the ancient Greeks' idea of Chaos. Beyond that critical point form and substance appear, just as the colours at the lowest infrared end of the colour spectrum suddenly appear out of darkness.

Within its own range of frequencies, the lowest or first realm thus formed is stable and real, and as detailed and complex as our own material one, its objects as solid to the beings who dwell in it as material ones are to us. When the vibrational rate rises above that range it eventually reaches a second critical point at which the next realm occurs, similar in some ways and different in others. The third, fourth, fifth, and so on occur within their vibrational rate ranges in the same way. Some ancient Chinese esotericists counted eleven such realms, but I believe there may be many more. What's more, on earth we humans of flesh and blood see only a small fraction of all that exists on the material sphere and in the material universe in which we live. There are large numbers of objects and beings of many kinds, of or associated with the material energy/substance, that humans can't see: its ghosts and devils and demons, its nature spirits and its gods great and small. Although the collective consciousness of the material sphere has detailed knowledge of Earth's other spheres, few people other than shamans ever experience the other spheres directly, or even believe in them, although science is opening up to the possibility of parallel universes as the secrets of the subatomic universe are probed. Some of the beings of other realms may be as ignorant of us as we are of them. Those realms with the lowest vibrational rate tend to have smaller, denser particles maintained with greater tension and force than those with higher rates, so they form dense, heavy, concentrated, very stable substances. Their planets have high gravity, their stars are far apart, and change strongly resisted. Those of the highest vibrational rates are lighter, less dense, occupy more space with less distance between objects in space, more mutable and more volatile. Magic happens much more readily on the higher planets, with many forms mutable or ephemeral. The forms tend to be more diverse too.

Our planet has seven spheres and the moon has five. The 'aquareal' sphere (I coined that name for it because it is liquid in character and has a clear, cool aqua light about it) exists between the aerial and the material spheres of the moon and has no earthly counterpart, while the moon has no counterparts for the Earths's Hadean, astral or aetheral spheres. Both have Tartarean, material, aerial and celestial spheres, although there are no material plants and animals on the moon's material surface.

For more detail, look at the diagram overleaf and its legend on the following pages.

An explanation of the relationships of the spheres of the Earth and Moon.

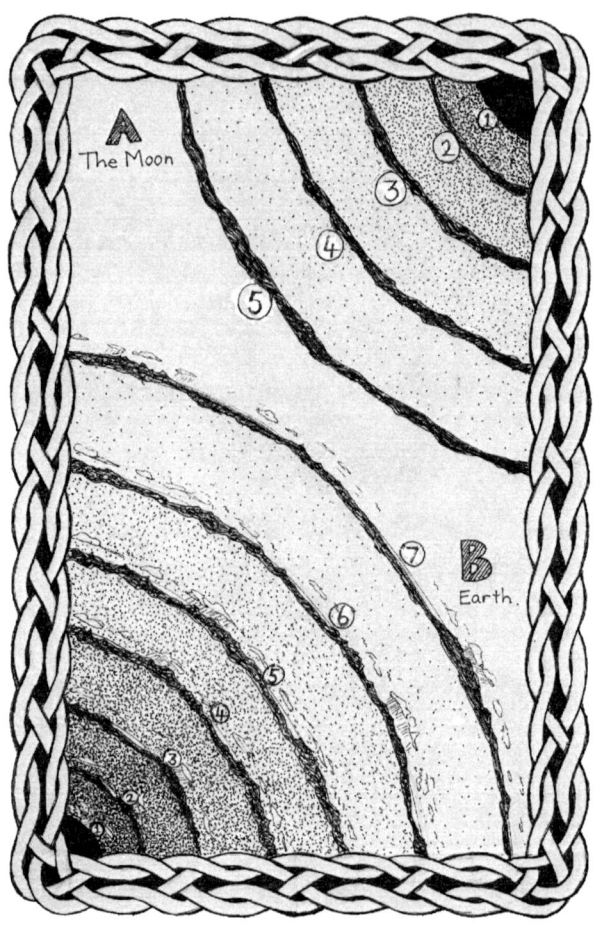

A.(1). The Moon's Tartarean Sphere.

The moon's focal feminine consciousness is within it, equally attuned to all her five spheres. Its surface is populated by mega-beings (Titans) whose function is the mediation of archetypes from the collective planetary consciousness to keep our planet's repertoire of forms and motifs up to date and keeping us compatible with mentality where ever in the universe it occurs. Shakespeares's Titania, the faerie queen in A Midsummer night's Dream, was of this sphere.

(2). The Moon's Material Sphere

This is the moon as we of Earth know it. It is the part we see waxing and waning when we look up into the sky, especially at night. It is inhabited only by aerial and aethereal beings from the moon and a few aerial, astral and aethereal beings from the earth, with the occasional material visitor since the first moon landing. Eventually it will be home to material beings, mostly diminutives from the moon's other spheres which will terraform it over the next few thousand years.

(3). The Moon's Aquareal Sphere

Soul beings exist here, winged diminutives more variable in appearance and function than those of the aerial sphere. They are rainbowed in colour and like liquids in their interrelationships.

(4). The Moon's Aereal Sphere

This is the most populous, most energetically active sphere of the moon, with a rapidly evolving fauna and flora, and large numbers of winged faeries. Most of their plant and animal forms were derived magically from resonant forms of earthly plants and animals, taken from various earthly spheres, but they at once come under the moon's own natural enchantment and take on lunar characteristics that distinguish them completely from the originals.

(5). The Moon's Celestial Sphere

This is the moon's outermost sphere, where moon devas, totem beings, and devils (not the malefic kind) dwell. Their function is to regulate the evolution of species and the generation of cultures and civilizations within the five spheres of the moon. The first male faerie, formed with the cooperation of the earth, appears here and functions as the moon's 'king'. His wedding to the Tartarean 'Titania' takes several thousand years and populates the vacant spheres between them with a full complement of planetary (lunar, that is) gods, devas, elementals and so on, all with the distinctive qualities of the faeries of the moon.

B. (1). The Earth's Tartarean Sphere

Within it is the seat of the planetary consciousness, charged with its logos and potent with cosmic memory and cosmic awareness—she answers to the name of Gaia, sometimes in the form of a rather sweet natured octopus. On its surface are Titans, well known from ancient Greek mythology. Dark, deep and distant, it's a world of archetypal beings, procedures and events.

(2). The Earth's Hadean Sphere

Hades, the Underworld, well-known by a variety of names to many cultures including the ancient Romans, is described in some detail in Virgil's Aeneid. Heroes and the virtuous dead were said to enjoy honour and privileges there, while unworthy men and women would find hardship and suffering. Its beings have a rich, tarry or oily feel; they sometimes show you glowing stones and dank, craggy landscapes.

(3). The Earth's Material Sphere

That part of it which is visible, audible, tangible, smellable and tastable to human beings needs no description. Beyond the ranges of our sensory array are energy substrates which resonate with the substances of the astral, hadean and some other spheres at least under some conditions, well enough to sustain impressions sufficiently well for astral beings (some ghosts, some discarnate souls, some nature spirits for example), to exist permanently as a kind of daughter culture, for aethereal beings to make brief appearances to gifted seers, for aerial beings such as faeries to be sustained in certain energized areas, such as protected gardens and natural places, and in the upper atmosphere, and for celestials to exist within it only under ritually controlled conditions which are sometimes risky for both invoker and invokee. These peripheral substrates facilitate exchanges of energies and beings between one sphere and the others, via the peripheral substrates of the other spheres, which would include matter-resonant substrates which would permit material beings to form resonant forms on those spheres through which they could be perceived, thus enabling shamans from our sphere to visit the others in the spirit.

(4). The Earth's Astral Sphere

Our nearest neighbour in character if not actually in distance (Hades is a little closer on the inner side), the astral sphere is often the next home for people who have died after a lifetime or several lifetimes on the material sphere. A parallel world to our own in many ways, we have always had and still have an uneasy relationship with some of the beings of the astral planet, which has occasionally erupted in hostility. It seems to me that we squabble like siblings. It appears as a clear or hazily coloured substance when seen on the material sphere and sometimes leaves a faintly chalky, slightly acrid odour or taste in the air.

(5). The Earth's Aerial Sphere

This is where Shintoists, ancient Germanic pagans and some Voudun nature spirit mediators focus their attention, and its beings sometimes communicate with us on the material sphere via the shifting shapes of clouds, which give them their best environment from which to commune with this sphere. They sometimes project quite spectacular visions for gifted seers of our sphere to see, hanging in the air at about the level of the clouds, of translucent, silky, gorgeously robed beings, sometime winged, sometimes with rainbows shimmering through them, and of course, our faeries have their colonies there.

(6). The Earth's Aethereal Sphere

This is the zone of the Valkyries, magical dwarves and giants, and the Pied Piper, of magicians who appear, interact dazzlingly with some terrestials, who often least expect it, and then vanish. Stark moral messages and magical gifts (and thefts) reach us from there. Its beings often appear as shiny apparitions, with a golden light about them. There may be a taste of honey about it, which is sometimes cloying. Gongs and Hawaiian guitars, harps and xylophones and small bells are characteristic of the aethereal sphere. In character it resembles Hades.

(7). The Earth's Celestial Sphere

Called Elysium by the Greeks and Hell by the Germanic peoples, the Celestial Sphere is the abode of the gods of the Earth, their priesthoods and courts, and their devotees who may have led pious lives on any or several of the other spheres of the Earth. The Celestial angels live here, and its visitors include cosmic angels and other beings, and the gods, devas, devils and so on of other planets as well. Its beings appearing to terrestrial shamans appear to be made of the same substance flames are made of but which does not flicker as flames do, gives out no heat, and is sometimes very radiant. Its beings are psychically very intense. The animal-headed gods and some dragons are found there.